IMAGES
of America

20TH-CENTURY RETAILING IN DOWNTOWN GRAND RAPIDS

IMAGES
of America

20TH-CENTURY RETAILING IN DOWNTOWN GRAND RAPIDS

Michael Hauser and Marianne Weldon

ARCADIA
PUBLISHING

Published by Arcadia Publishing
Charleston, South Carolina

Library of Congress Control Number: 2014933629

For all general information, please contact Arcadia Publishing:
Telephone 843-853-2070
Fax 843-853-0044
E-mail sales@arcadiapublishing.com
For customer service and orders:
Toll-Free 1-888-313-2665

Visit us on the Internet at www.arcadiapublishing.com

CONTENTS

ACKNOWLEDGMENTS

We gratefully acknowledge the assistance of the following individuals: Alex Forist and the staff of the Grand Rapids Public Museum, Tim Gleisner and the staff of the Grand Rapids Public Library, Judy Horn at the Ella Sharp Museum in Jackson, Michigan, and Robert Goodrich.

Additionally, we would like to thank our editors, Liz Gurley and Jacel Egan, for their guidance and support.

INTRODUCTION

For many folks, recalling the era when downtown Grand Rapids was a mecca for West Michigan shoppers evokes memories of riding the bus downtown, window-shopping, ogling the holiday decor, visiting the "real" Santa, watching the elevators *whoosh* between floors, and listening to the *clickety-clack* of the escalators.

Others may remember being a member of the teen board, attending a style show in one of the department store dining rooms, freezing on Monroe Avenue while watching the Santa Claus Parade, playing the latest top-40 tunes, or purchasing a first pet from one of the dime stores.

Back in the 1950s—the heyday for downtown retailing—venturing to downtown Grand Rapids was a daylong adventure. Besides offering over one million square feet of retailing, the area also boasted many nearby restaurants and half a dozen first-run movie palaces.

Monroe Avenue was home to three homegrown department stores (Herpolsheimer's, Steketee's, and Wurzburg's), as well as Jacobson's, Sears Roebuck & Company, four large dime stores (W.T. Grant Company, H.L. Green Company, S.S. Kresge Company, and F.W. Woolworth Company), and scores of specialty stores.

Names such as Herpolsheimer, Herkner, Houseman, May, Preusser, Steketee, and Wurzburg still resonate with the citizenry today because of the active role these businesspeople contributed to the arts and culture of Grand Rapids. Today, the consolidation of the retail industry and the proliferation of big-box retailers have severely diminished the community-giving aspect that was the hallmark of the aforementioned retailers and have made today's shopping experience far less personal.

Many of the early merchants that dominated Monroe Avenue, who were immigrants of various origins, could trace their roots to small dry goods stores of the 19th century. As the city prospered, so did these merchants who supplied durable goods to the growing population.

Following World War II, the migration to neighborhood and suburban areas gripped Grand Rapids, just as it had elsewhere around the country. The earliest local shopping areas were West Leonard, Burton Heights, Madison Square, Town and Country, Gaslight Village, Breton Village, Creston Heights, Galewood, and Standale. Roger's Plaza, the area's first enclosed shopping mall in 1960, was a revelation. Although the downtown stores held their own, it was not until the opening of Eastbrook Mall in 1967 and Woodland Mall in 1968 that downtown started to experience a serious drop-off in business and guest traffic.

In some respects, the large department stores cannibalized themselves. Wurzburg's opened branches in Southland Center (1964), Eastbrook Mall (1966), and North Kent Mall (1970). Herpolsheimer's acquired the former Southland Center store from Wurzburg's in 1976, and Steketee's opened a branch at Eastbrook Mall in 1967.

The real death knell for downtown retailing occurred in 1971, when the new owners of Wurzburg's announced they would close the venerable Monroe Avenue department store. Wurzburg's for decades had been Grand Rapids's version of the J.L. Hudson Company of Detroit. Wurzburg's operated a large 10-story edifice, produced the Santa Claus Parade, created magical animated window displays, featured elaborate holiday decor, and was the largest advertiser in town. Following its departure, Herpolsheimer's skated along until 1990, and Steketee's until 1998, although both stores were shadows of their former selves. Most of the specialty stores closed in the 1970s and were replaced with smaller niche merchants. A few of the vanguard retailers have survived downtown, including Preusser Jewelers, Groskopf's Luggage & Gifts, and Reynolds & Son Sporting Goods.

During the demolition of the famed Wurzburg store, a foreman from Capitol Lumber and Wrecking stated to the media that "there is nothing structurally wrong with it—it is a beautiful building!" Frederick Schoeck, Wurzburg's longtime president, stated, "I think it is stupid! My life's work is ruined. We built a big store with the help of Sperry and Hutchinson. Now it is gone. I don't want to say any more!" Back in the 1970s, community leaders did not have the foresight to believe that these former retail edifices could evolve into mixed-use facilities.

My (coauthor Michael Hauser) fascination with downtown and its wide range of retail began in the mid-1950s when my parents enrolled me in summer classes at the Grand Rapids Public Museum. Once I learned the ropes, I rode the bus downtown on my own, filling my mind with images of the various styles of architecture and neon signage that I could see out the window. Once home, I would create my own version of the stores, restaurants, and theaters in sketchbooks. In the late 1950s, our family treat was to occasionally take the bus downtown together on Friday evenings when the stores were open late. We would window-shop, rotate dining at the dime store lunch counters, and end the evening with a movie.

As a student at Central High School, I would walk downtown each afternoon to catch the bus home, hoping to one day be able to work in this environment. My dream was fulfilled while I was attending college, when I held various jobs at Steketee's and three of the remaining downtown movie palaces. Following college, my professional career began with a marketing position at Herpolsheimer's.

Marianne and I have attempted here to provide a glimpse of the great retailers we once had downtown. Obviously, we have only scratched the surface; in some cases, there was simply insufficient information or images available to include the hundreds of merchants the core city once supported.

Downtown Grand Rapids today is bustling with commerce, fueled by sports, entertainment, the courts, education, and hospitality. We will never again have the critical mass of retail that created such fond memories for so many thousands of Grand Rapidians. However, thanks to the tireless efforts of the staff and volunteers at the Grand Rapids Public Museum and the Grand Rapids Public Library, those glorious memories will live on in perpetuity.

One

THE HERPOLSHEIMER COMPANY

DELIVERING THE GOODS, 1920s. As times and technology evolved, horse-drawn delivery wagons gave way to electric vehicles and, eventually, to trucks. Having parcels of merchandise delivered by a Herpolsheimer's delivery associate was a status symbol in the early part of the 20th century. (Courtesy Collections of the Grand Rapids Public Museum.)

The Herpolsheimer Store. GRAND RAPIDS, MICH.

MONROE AND OTTAWAY AVENUES, 1910S. Herpolsheimer's was founded in 1870 by William G. Herpolsheimer, who fulfilled his pre–Civil War dream of opening a successful dry goods emporium. That same year, he became acquainted with Carl G.A. Voigt, who also wished to be part of this new venture. Following William's stint in the Union army, the two joined forces to create the Voigt-Herpolsheimer Dry Goods Company. (Courtesy Michael Hauser.)

GRAND RAPIDS, MICH

HERPOLSHEIMER'S SEVEN-STORY STORE, 1910S. William Herpolsheimer's son Henry joined the concern at an early age, and he and his father purchased a site at Monroe and Ottawa Avenues following a fire in 1902. The Herpolsheimers decided to go it alone, dissolving the partnership with Voigt. Henry assumed active management as his father gradually retired. Henry's son Arthur joined the firm following his father's death and managed the store until it was acquired by Hahn Department Stores in 1929. Hahn Stores became Allied Stores Corporation in 1935 and owned Herpolsheimer's until 1987. (Courtesy Michael Hauser.)

SHOWING PATRIOTIC COLORS, 1925. The seven-story portion of Herpolsheimer's store at 101 Monroe Avenue was completed in 1904, with a 10-story addition opening in 1911. The first skyscraper in Grand Rapids, the store featured an observatory on the roof that provided a panoramic view of the growing city. The building boasted six passenger elevators, which could barely handle the crowds, and four additional elevators were installed. (Courtesy Collections of the Grand Rapids Public Museum.)

TOWER ADDITION, 1912. A barometer of Herpolsheimer's rapid growth was the store's switchboard system. In 1917, the exchange was located on the seventh floor and consisted of a two-position board and a Michigan Bell board receiver. By the 1920s, the exchange moved to the sixth floor, and 50 additional phones were added. In 1939, the exchange moved to the 10th floor and featured a three-position board with 200 phones, 50 exchange phones, 23 incoming lines, and 10 outgoing lines. (Courtesy Michael Hauser.)

THE BOYS' DEPARTMENT, 1910s. In the 1920s, one of the store's advertisements proclaimed Herpolsheimer's "part of the bone and sinew of Grand Rapids. An entirely local mercantile institution expanding in step with the city's growth!" The store also boasted of its artistic corner in the new Art and Gift Shop, which was "the talk of the town!" (Courtesy Michael Hauser.)

WOMEN'S POWDER ROOM, 1914. The ladies' restrooms on the eighth floor were spacious and well appointed in comparison with today's cramped quarters. Features included mahogany walls, wicker furniture, plenty of lounge chairs and sofas, and desks stocked with stationery and pens for letter writing. (Courtesy Michael Hauser.)

TEA ROOM, 1910s. Herpolsheimer's Tea Room, located high atop the store, was both a culinary and social destination. The room was awash with natural light from the many windows surrounding the room. Tables were adorned with crisp, white linens, fresh flowers, and fine china and serve ware. In 1929, the Tea Room moved to the second floor. (Courtesy Michael Hauser.)

For Your Convenience
AN EVER GREATER STORE

*T*he variety of services offered you at Herpolsheimer's would fill a small book. May we, at this time call to your attention these few, which will likely prove of the most frequent convenience to you . . . The Service Desk, on the Street Floor, where you may mail letters, buy money orders, check parcels or belongings. The Gift Wrapping Department where you may have the gifts you have selected wrapped in accordance with the occasion . . . The Tea Room on the Second Floor, is an ideal spot for relaxing luncheon . . . The attractive Marine Bar on the Street Floor for a delightful quick luncheon . . . The Modern Beauty Salon, on the Second Floor . . . A group of home services such as furniture repairing, re-upholstering, custom drapery making . . . the helpful suggestions of our Interior Decorators. In each department you will find the largest assortments in Western Michigan . . . the highest quality of merchandise at the lowest possible cost.

HERPOLSHEIMER CO.
GRAND RAPIDS 2, MICH.

CHARMING GUESTS WITH DISTINCTIVE SERVICES, 1940s. Herpolsheimer's was known for its extensive customer services. "Ruth Kent" was the store's personal shopping service, which even had its own radio program on WKZO five days a week. (Courtesy Michael Hauser.)

A Visit from St. Nicholas

*L*ong before the night before Christmas, jolly old St. Nick paid us a special visit. He left us lots and lots of toys . . . the kind boys and girls like best. He knows, too, because he gets so many letters from children just like you. This is your invitation to come in and see them. It will be loads of fun . . . and you never can tell . . . Santa may be here to greet you!

"HERPOLSHEIMER'S TOYLAND"
Seventh Floor

VINTAGE HOLIDAY ADVERTISEMENT, 1940. Santa's tradition with Herpolsheimer's dates to 1916, when he first appeared in the seventh-floor toy department. In later years, at the new location, Santa shared space with Rudolph the talking reindeer. Children could speak with Rudy, rub his nose (which lit up), and for a quarter receive a surprise gift, which flew down an adjoining slide. (Courtesy Michael Hauser.)

Herpolsheimer News

Published monthly by Herpolsheimer Co., Grand Rapids, Mich.

AUTUMN, 1923

EMPLOYEE PUBLICATION, 1923. Publications such as this edition of the *Herpolsheimer News* informed store associates of various happenings within the company. The *Herpolsheimer News* was published under various names from the 1920s through the 1970s, and columns in this publication described activities on each floor of the store. (Courtesy Michael Hauser.)

Herpolsheimer's HIGH-LIGHTS

VOL. 2, No. 5.　　　　GRAND RAPIDS, MICHIGAN　　　　MARCH, 1947

WILLMARK "100" CLUB

The Willmark Shopping Service is an organization that sends out "shoppers" to various department stores to ascertain the alertness of the salesperson, checking on her manner of approach, personality, courtesy, and so on.

This month we are presenting Herpolsheimer's "Willmark Winners" for 1946, as well as those who have won such honors so far this year.

Congratulations to each of you, and we are looking forward to publishing the pictures of other winners as the weeks roll by.

Song of the Tube Room

Did you ever work in the Tube Room of
a big department store,
Where the carriers came down with lots
of noise
For a dollar in change or more,
Where you hand out bags of money,
To the clerks who come to the door,
And you check them in, again at night,
With fifteen dollars—or more?

You may take in a sum of three hundred,
Or cash a check for four,
But always a smile, not just once in a
while,
For two hundred clerks or more.
If ever you come in to see us,
You'll agree we have quite a chore,
To make the whole system run smoothly,
In a Big Department Store!
　　　Mrs. E. Bayle—Tube Room.

Come on, folks, High-Lights is YOUR paper, so why not give us some of your poems, essays or bits of philosophy—or even your favorite lines from other authors. We WANT your contributions!

THEY HIT THE JACKPOT

Above—Members of the "100 Club" for 1946 include, left to right: Kathleen Hoogerland, Stationery; Victoria Dempsey, Art Needlework; Lottie Kaminski, Daytime Dresses; Mrs. Lila Stephens, Linens, 4th Floor; Harriette Chertos, Cosmetics. Emma Haubiel, Linens, 4th Floor, was not present when the picture was taken.

Below—Members of the 1947 group so far are, left to right: Ruth Zaroff, Lingerie; Fontilla Esdair, Hosiery, and Betty Cowan, Cotton Shop, all from the Downstairs Store. Blanch Clifford, Infants' Wear, is also a member of the 1947 group.

MORE EMPLOYEE NEWS, 1947. This issue focused on the store's female softball team, known as the Herp's Twerps. The store sponsored sports teams that competed with other city merchant teams in baseball, basketball, bowling, and golf. Other news covered employee birthdays, anniversaries, engagements, weddings, vacations, and sick bay items. (Courtesy Michael Hauser.)

BROWSING IN THE BOOK DEPARTMENT, 1938. Displaying diverse interests, the woman on the left is reading the Bible, while her friend on the right is glancing at *Hansel and Gretel.* Herpolsheimer's popular book department was located on the second floor. The store also had a lending library, whereby a guest could rent a book at a cost of 25¢ for a two-week period. (Courtesy Grand Rapids History & Special Collections, Archives, Grand Rapids Public Library.)

THE WORLD OF DOLLS, 1938. This young lady is trying to convince her mother to purchase an Effanbee doll. Effanbee was known for its wildly popular Patsy doll, which was one of the first dolls to have a wardrobe created specifically for her. This doll also had a patented neck joint that allowed the doll to pose and stand alone. (Courtesy Grand Rapids History & Special Collections, Archives, Grand Rapids Public Library.)

VISITING SANTA IN TOYLAND, 1941. These two youngsters have just received issues of Dell Comics' *Radior* series from Kris Kringle. Each of the five characters in this series had their own 16-page section devoted to them, something rare in comics at that time. (Courtesy Grand Rapids History & Special Collections, Archives, Grand Rapids Public Library.)

FAMILIES ENTHRALLED WITH TRAINS, 1943. Herpolsheimer's toy department promoted itself as the *right* place to buy the *right* toys at the *right* price and with the *right* service. Each holiday season, the department was elaborately decorated with a new theme. (Courtesy Grand Rapids History & Special Collections, Archives, Grand Rapids Public Library.)

OTTAWA AVENUE FACADE, 1940s. Herpolsheimer's was a busy store in the 1940s, and its most famous employee was none other than Betty Bloomer, later known to millions as First Lady Betty Ford. Ms. Bloomer was employed at the store as a model from 1932 to 1936. In 1941, she was appointed assistant fashion coordinator, and from 1942 to 1947 she was the fashion coordinator. (Courtesy Michael Hauser.)

OTTAWA AVENUE GARDEN STORE, 1940s. Before the advent of specialty stores and big-box retailers, department stores like Herpolsheimer's were all things to all people, carrying everything from a spool of thread to grand pianos. Seen here is the Ottawa Avenue Garden Center, selling trees, plants, shrubs, tools, and seeds. (Courtesy Michael Hauser.)

HERPOLSHEIMER'S FAMOUS MARINE BAR, 1943. The Marine Bar was one of several popular spots to dine at Herpolsheimer's. The Shoppers' Special was a favorite of many: for 30¢, one could enjoy a summer-sausage sandwich, orange sherbet, and a choice of coffee or iced tea; for 55¢, one could order grilled calves liver with a strip of bacon and cauliflower with au gratin sauce on toast. (Courtesy Michael Hauser.)

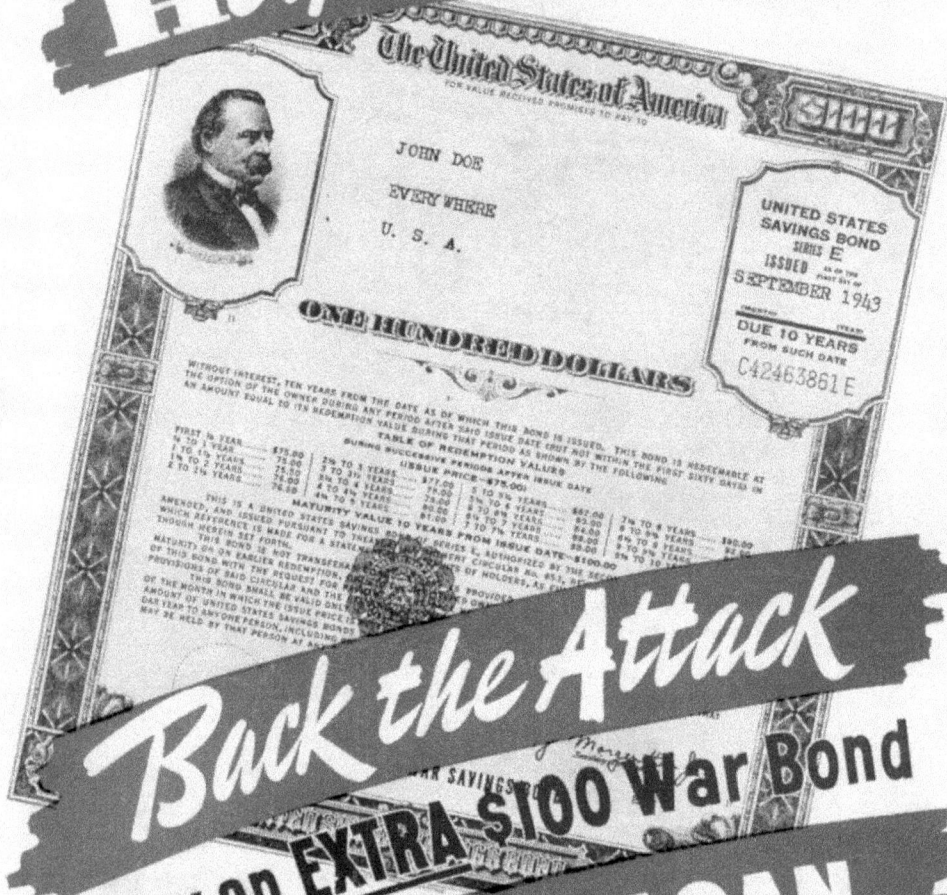

HERPOLSHEIMER'S WAR EFFORTS, 1943. Like many department stores, Herpolsheimer's played an important role with the sale of war bonds during World War II. Special Victory Booths were set up in various locations of the store. During one memorable promotion, the stars of the Warner Bros. film *The Desert Song* appeared in person, and those that purchased a war bond received an autographed photograph. (Courtesy Michael Hauser.)

OTTAWA AVENUE APPLIANCE STORE, 1920S. Herpolsheimer's appliance department staged a coup in 1947 by producing a half-mile-long parade to welcome the RCA Television Caravan. The parade included clowns, elephants, floats, and a calliope. To celebrate Television Week, live remotes were broadcast from the store three times daily with local celebrities and politicians. (Courtesy Michael Hauser.)

COMPLETED APPLIANCE STORE, 1930S. Herpolsheimer's home store introduced the House Beautiful Studios shop in 1939. Store buyer Nona Dumas traversed the New York showrooms to fill this corner of the fifth floor with unusual gifts that included lamps, pottery, glassware, and accessories. (Courtesy Michael Hauser.)

LOUIS STREET PARKING GARAGE, 1930s. This structure at Louis and Ottawa Avenues had previously been utilized for Herpolsheimer's wholesale division, which moved here in 1915 from the main store. All reserve stock, as well as the floor-covering and drapery workrooms, had been housed here. With downtown parking becoming scarce by the 1930s, management felt the need to convert the structure for that purpose. (Courtesy Michael Hauser.)

MOVING SALE IN THE BASEMENT YARD GOODS DEPARTMENT, 1949. Herpolsheimer's Basement Store began in the original 1904 structure at Monroe and Ottawa Avenues. This store within a store featured almost all of the departments one would find in the upstairs store, from clothing for the entire family to linens and home furnishings. There was also a malt bar located in the Basement Store. (Courtesy Michael Hauser.)

MOVING SALE IN MEN'S FURNISHINGS, 1949. The Basement Store would occasionally receive closeouts from major resources as well as from other national retailers. At times, these deals could not be advertised, and in some cases the labels were cut out. Receiving and marking rooms for the entire store were located in the sub-basement of the building. (Courtesy Michael Hauser.)

MOVING SALE IN BASEMENT LINEN DEPARTMENT, 1949. These shoppers are perusing a closeout sale on huckaback towels (at 35¢ each). Huckaback towels featured a linen-cotton blend that lent itself to embroidery of any type. The beauty of these towels was their versatility; they could be used as a guest towel, kitchen towel, or a tea towel. (Courtesy Michael Hauser.)

THE PORTER BLOCK, 1940s. The block of buildings on the left in this image would eventually be demolished for the construction of the new, ultramodern Herpolsheimer's. Businesses that were displaced included Wilson's Lunch, Raymer's Books, Hager's, and Miller's Foods. The project was announced on April 2, 1947. (Courtesy Michael Hauser.)

EXECUTIVE SIDEWALK SUPERINTENDENTS, 1948. These executives are watching construction of the new Herpolsheimer's from a cozy vantage point. Allied Stores retained the Boston architectural firm of Perry, Shaw & Hepburn to design this modern structure. Additionally, Allied corporate architect George Ely assisted with the team. (Courtesy Michael Hauser.)

26

HERPOLSHEIMER'S NEW STORE, 1949. Signage around all three sides of the future store salute a number of the city's leading nonprofit organizations. "Building with confidence in Greater Grand Rapids" was the theme. Herpolsheimer's had a long history of supporting local arts organizations. (Courtesy Michael Hauser.)

OVERVIEW FROM GILBERT BUILDING ROOF, 1949. George Ely, Allied Stores corporate architect, developed a unique contribution to the design of Herpolsheimer's: a suspended grill ceiling. This was devised to obscure the mechanical area above the ceiling and to diffuse the illumination so that it would approximate daylight. Ely also created a band system of alternating storage and service floors that existed as half floors between the selling floors. (Courtesy Michael Hauser.)

DIVISION AVENUE EXTERIOR OF NEW STORE, 1949. America's state-of-the-art department store opened on November 15, 1949. Herpolsheimer's featured the latest in guest conveniences, including floating escalators, indoor parking, wider aisles, better illumination, and multiple dining options. The new store was composed of three selling floors and two basements and contained 347,500 square feet of space. (Courtesy Grand Rapids History & Special Collections, Archives, Grand Rapids Public Library.)

CUSTOMER SERVICE AT NEW STORE, 1949. Grand Rapids Store Equipment received the contract to produce showcases and fixtures for the new Herpolsheimer's. Allied Stores committed $3 million to construct this edifice. The store was located at the epicenter of the city with the distinct address of No. 1 Monroe Avenue, No. 1 Division Avenue, and No. 1 Fulton Street. (Courtesy Collections of the Grand Rapids Public Museum.)

ENTERING THE BABY BOOM, 1950S. For decades, the Kent Room dining room on the second floor was *the* spot to dine and enjoy the weekly style shows. It was also a popular noontime destination for businesspeople, politicians, and local celebrities. Classic menu items that stood the test of time included the shrimp salad, chicken potpie, blueberry muffins, and the decadent pecan fudge ball. (Courtesy Michael Hauser.)

MOVING ON UP, 1960. In 1968, Herpolsheimer's became the first department store in Michigan licensed to serve liquor by the glass (in the store's Kent Room). Another novelty at this time was that guests could say, "Charge it, please," for their adult beverages. The store also added an afternoon happy hour. (Courtesy Michael Hauser.)

ASSISTING CUSTOMERS, 1949. These crowds proved that Herpolsheimer's lived up to its hype for the new store "where thousands shop for better things!" The store continually added new brands and shops throughout the 1950s. (Courtesy Michael Hauser.)

ALWAYS ON THE MOVE, 1949. Herpolsheimer's fashion departments were always a step ahead, from the upscale Vogue and I. Miller Salons to the city's largest fur salon and even the Basement Store, whose buyers scoured the markets for store exclusives. The store's Wednesday luncheon style shows were a cherished tradition for generations of guests. (Courtesy Michael Hauser.)

ELABORATE HOLIDAY WINDOW, 1950S. Herpolsheimer's featured the largest display window in the United States. Facing Division Avenue, the three-story window, when not displaying a large American flag, was utilized to showcase elaborate holiday displays, seasonal promotions, and public-service displays. (Courtesy Michael Hauser.)

ESCALATOR QUEUE ON MAIN FLOOR, 1949. Herpolsheimer's One Shop on the second floor was the exclusive home of Eisenberg Originals, an upscale line of women's clothing and jewelry. Another upscale designer, Jacques Fath, was also represented in this chic corner of the store, as was Mademoiselle Shoes. (Courtesy Michael Hauser.)

EXCITEMENT ABOUNDS AT THE NEW STORE, 1949. The pleasing soft brown walls, the grey oak showcases, and the acres of merchandise drew hordes of guests to Herpolsheimer's new home at Monroe and Division Avenues. In later years, added guest conveniences included a free-parking program and a hotline that allowed guests to connect directly with the president's office from strategically placed red telephones in the store. (Courtesy Michael Hauser.)

BOW TIES, ALWAYS IN STYLE, 1949. The "most beautiful store" of its time in 1949, Herpolsheimer's was ready for additional makeovers within a decade of its opening. Several floors were remodeled in 1959 and again in 1969. Retail, after all, is all about constant change. The 1969 renovation saw major changes to the accessories area, intimate apparel department, and the Kent Room dining room. (Courtesy Michael Hauser.)

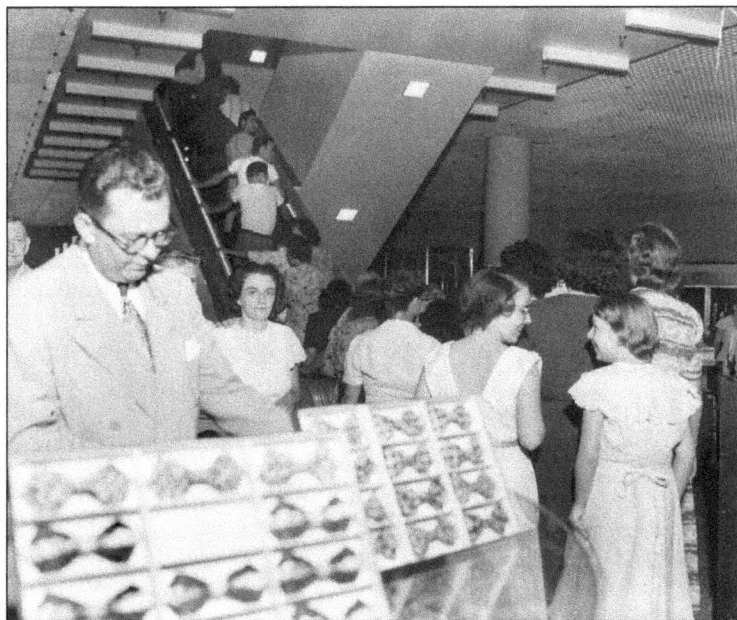

HERPOLSHEIMER'S FAMOUS ELEVATED TRAIN, 1976. Installed in 1949, Herpolsheimer's Louis Street level-three car monorail was capable of transporting 24 children at a time, suspended from a 400-foot-long track. The train took on different personas through the years: in the 1950s, it was Santa's Express; in the 1960s, it was rechristened Santa's Space Capsule; and in the 1970s, it evolved into the Caterpillar Express. The train stopped running in 1983 for the construction of the City Centre mall and was resurrected as the Dino Express in 1985. (Courtesy Grand Rapids History & Special Collections, Archives, Grand Rapids Public Library.)

SUCCESSOR TO THE CHRISTMAS CLUB, 1975. This holiday money promotion began in the 1970s as a way to assist families with their holiday purchases. Any items purchased in October would not be billed until February. Another Herpolsheimer tradition that began in 1972 was Breakfast with Santa in the Kent Room. This program included a visit from Santa and a show featuring magician extraordinaire June Horowitz. (Courtesy Michael Hauser.)

YET ANOTHER NEW ERA, 1985. In October 1985, the name Herp's was retired, and the company reopened its downtown store in the City Centre mall, rechristening itself "Herpolsheimer's." (The name was shortened to Herp's in the 1970s.) City Centre was created by gutting the original Herpolsheimer's and the adjacent Gantos store. Because of consolidations within the retail industry, Herpolsheimer's merged with Block's of Indianapolis in 1987. Later that year, it became part of the Lazarus chain. By 1990, the store closed, ending a 120-year tradition. (Courtesy Michael Hauser.)

Two

PAUL STEKETEE AND SONS

STEKETEE'S DELIVERY TRUCK, 1920S. Steketee's ended its horse-and-wagon delivery service in 1914 with the purchase of an overland delivery vehicle, thus paving the way for gasoline-powered vehicles. Delivery schedules at this time called for two runs in the morning and another pair of runs in the afternoon. (Courtesy Collections of the Grand Rapids Public Museum.)

CORNER OF STEKETEE'S READY-TO-WEAR SECTION
GRAND RAPIDS MICH

WOMEN'S DEPARTMENTS, THIRD FLOOR, 1910s. Steketee's was founded by Paul Steketee, an emigrant from the Netherlands, who arrived in Grand Rapids in 1850. Steketee and John Doornink collaborated in 1862, opening a dry goods store on Monroe Avenue that operated for a decade before being destroyed by fire. Following the fire, Doornink left the business, and Steketee recruited his brother Andris to join the firm. (Courtesy Michael Hauser.)

Corner Ionia and Fountain Streets, Grand Rapids. Mich., showing P. Steketee & Sons Building

IONIA AVENUE ENTRANCE, 1910. From 1878 to 1931, Steketee's also operated a wholesale business. In earlier days, when lumbering was at its peak, and continuing through World War I, the wholesale portion of the business was lucrative. With the advent of better transportation and an increasingly mobile shopping public, the retail portion of the business became more important, and the wholesale division was eliminated. (Courtesy Michael Hauser.)

36

STEKETEE'S EIGHT-STORY BUILDING AT 86 MONROE AVENUE, 1925. This portion of the store's downtown complex opened in 1916 and was hailed as being "thoroughly equipped with all of the latest features that go to make up the modern metropolitan business home!" After an addition in 1920 and the rebuilding of the adjacent Steketee's Men's Store in 1940, the downtown store totaled 194,000 square feet of space. (Courtesy Collections of the Grand Rapids Public Museum.)

MEN'S AND WOMEN'S FRAGRANCE WINDOW, 1920s. The advent of department stores such as Steketee's opened the door for wider distribution of fragrance and skin-care products for both men and women. As specific brands became better known, packaging of the product became just as integral. (Courtesy Collections of the Grand Rapids Public Museum.)

STYLISH DRESS WINDOWS ON MONROE AVENUE, 1938. This window-shopper is ogling the latest dress designs for the upcoming holiday season. In 1938, styles were for the most part soft, but as World War II approached, garments became much more tailored and businesslike. Hemlines rose, and waistline seams were accessorized with belts. (Courtesy Grand Rapids History & Special Collections, Archives, Grand Rapids Public Library.)

IONIA AVENUE ENTRANCE TO LINEN DEPARTMENT, 1927. Steketee's, like many retailers, operated its organization as if it were a family. Case in point is this passage from the employee manual: "True . . . we're in the retail business, selling things, but its people we're selling those things to. We ought to become 'people oriented.' If folks like us well enough, they'll be in to see us. Selling is a person-to-person relationship, and we can never afford to neglect the human aspect of merchandising." (Courtesy Collections of the Grand Rapids Public Museum.)

FOUNTAIN STREET ENTRANCE, 1998. The years following World War II saw tremendous growth for the company. Steketee's purchased the Lee and Cady Warehouse on Jefferson Avenue, and it became the new distribution center. In 1949, Grand Rapids Store Equipment installed new showcases and display units in the store. Air-conditioning was installed gradually, and by 1956 the entire downtown complex was fully air-conditioned. (Courtesy Michael Hauser.)

STEKETEE'S ASSOCIATES HOLD FORTH AT HOOVER DISPLAY, 1910s. The Hoover Vacuum Company drew up agreements with retailers like Steketee's to become dealerships for the company. The dealer then received a commission for each vacuum sold. Additionally, guests were offered a complimentary 10-day trial period to test the vacuum. (Courtesy Collections of the Grand Rapids Public Museum.)

Trade Winds

JUNE 1970   PAUL STEKETEE & SONS, CO.   Vol. 7 NO. 2

SHADES OF 1870

Note to all employees in 1970. Here are the office rules back in the 1870's:

Employees will daily sweep floors, dust the furniture and shelves.

Each day, fill lamps, clean chimneys, trim wicks, wash windows once a week.

Each clerk will bring in a bucket of water and a scuttle of coal daily.

Make your pens carefully. You may whittle nibs to your own taste.

The office will open at 7:00 AM and close at 8:00 PM daily except on the Sabbath, on which day it will remain closed. Each employee is expected to spend the Sabbath by attending church and contributing liberally to the cause of the Lord.

Men employees will be given an evening a week for courting purposes or two evenings a week if they go to church regularly.

After an employee has spent his hours of labor in the office he should spend his time reading the Bible and other good books.

Any employee who smokes Spanish Cigars, uses liquor in any form, gets shaved in the barber shop or frequents pool and public halls, will give me good reason to suspect his worth, intentions, integrity and honesty.

The employee who has performed his labors faithfully and without fault FOR A PERIOD OF FIVE YEARS and who has been thrifty and attentive to his religious duties will be given an INCREASE OF FIVE CENTS PER DAY, provided a just return in profit from the business permits it.

"It is easy to see why the employer would question the honesty of any employee caught smoking a Spanish Cigar or being shaved in the barber shop. He would know these luxuries could not come out of a nickel-a-day raise"!

--------------------From Hatters Chatter, Chicago

1.

STEKETEE'S IN-HOUSE NEWSLETTER, 1970. *Trade Winds* was the in-house publication for Steketee's employees. It was published under various nameplates from the 1930s through the 1980s. Each issue focused on company business and events, followed by employee news (organized floor by floor). Stories covered in this issue include promotions, retirements, vacations, and bowling-league scores. (Courtesy Michael Hauser.)

MONROE AVENUE EXTERIOR, 1998. Guest-friendly traditions abounded at Steketee's. These included a personal shopper, corporate gift consultant, free gift boxes, a baby registry, a bridal registry, gift certificates, and monogramming and engraving services. During the holidays, the store sponsored the annual Jaycees Shopping Spree for underprivileged children, organized a men's night lingerie show, and hosted Santa in the children's department. (Courtesy Michael Hauser.)

IONIA AVENUE FIRE ESCAPE, 1998. Steketee's joined the Frederick Atkins buying syndicate in 1944. Atkins was a nonprofit marketing organization that acted as a cooperative buying office for department stores such as Steketee's, who were not only members but also owned the organization. Atkins purchased merchandise, developed house brands, monitored supplies, prices, fashion trends, and facilitated reports and surveys for its members. (Courtesy Michael Hauser.)

42

MONROE AVENUE MEN'S STORE, 1998.
Steketee's was always known for its personal
service. If a guest wore clothing into the
store that needed a snagged button or
seam mended, associates took the items
up to the alterations department for repair
while the guest shopped. "Jane Stewart"
was the moniker for the store's personal
shopper. (Courtesy Michael Hauser.)

FOUNTAIN STREET AWNING, 1998. In 1985,
following several focus groups and results
from a consulting firm, Steketee's elected
to discontinue the china, glassware, gift,
housewares, stationery, lamp, and luggage
departments. Additionally, the much-
beloved Budget Store was to be eliminated,
as were the bridal and gift registries. Upon
completion of these closeouts, retail selling
area would account for 55,000 square feet
of space. (Courtesy Michael Hauser.)

STEKETEE'S FAMOUS MAIN FLOOR SCALE, 1998. This scale was a favorite spot for children to gather, as it was near the main-floor candy department. Nearby was a large grandfather clock that had been presented by Steketee's sales associates to the Steketee family in 1917 for display in the store. This clock symbolized the solidarity of the retailer, and for decades businesspeople and shoppers alike would be directed to "meet me at the clock at Stek's!" (Courtesy Michael Hauser.)

MONROE AVENUE NAMEPLATE, 1998. In 1987, the downtown store underwent a $4.5 million renovation, which was the final step in shifting the focus of the company from a full-line department store to a specialty retailer with emphasis on clothing and accessories. With this renovation, floors four through six and the basement were closed. The nameplates still adorn the Monroe Avenue facade of the building. (Courtesy Michael Hauser.)

CLOSING SALE, FIRST FLOOR, 1998. After 91 years of operation as a partnership, Steketee's was incorporated in 1953. The store was not only the last remaining department store downtown, it was also one of the last remaining independently owned department store chains in the United States. Five generations of Steketee family members had operated and managed the store for almost 100 years. (Courtesy Michael Hauser.)

CLOSING SALE, ELEVATOR BANK, 1998. Steketee's was sold in 1991 to the Dunlap Group of Fort Worth, Texas. Dunlap operated stores primarily in the South. With declining sales at the downtown store, Dunlap elected in 1996 to close the second and third floors and concentrate on women's apparel and accessories on the main floor. Thus, the children's, men's, lingerie, and linen departments were discontinued. (Courtesy Michael Hauser.)

FIXTURE SALE, SECOND FLOOR, 1998. Many folks felt that the decision to eliminate a number of nonfashion departments through the years was ironic given that Steketee's had for years called itself "the home store." Other areas to close included the large beauty salon on the third floor and the contract interiors department. (Courtesy Michael Hauser.)

WATERFALL RACKS AND T-STANDS, SECOND FLOOR, 1998. The rise and fall of this once great store can be seen in the employment data. Steketee's began with a handful of employees in 1862 and by 1887 had 17 associates. At its peak in the 1940s, the downtown store employed 400 associates. By 1998, when the downtown store closed, it was down to 20 employees. (Courtesy Michael Hauser.)

VERTICAL TRAVEL BETWEEN FLOORS, 1998. Elevators were the primary mode of travel for guests at Steketee's for decades. There were four Otis cars with friendly operators in the main building that were graced with glass doors and brass interior fixtures up until 1961, when the cars were automated. Escalators were not installed in the downtown store until 1957, and those only serviced the first three floors. (Courtesy Michael Hauser.)

THE GRAND DAME OF MONROE AVENUE, 1998. Following the store's closure in 1998, there were several ambitious plans for the building to become a mixed-use development. There was even one scenario in 2000 for the structure to become a carrier hotel, housing telecommunications firms and Internet providers. (Courtesy Michael Hauser.)

ONE DAY SPECIALS All Stores Open **9:00 a.m. Wednesday, September 28**

Steketee's ANNIVERSARY SALE

September 28 through **October 9**

A FINAL SALE, 1998. Here is the cover of a direct mail piece for one of the final sales at Steketee's. Happily, in 2004, Blue Cross Blue Shield of Michigan decided to consolidate its regional office and move into the renovated Steketee's Building. At the time of reopening, an Independent Bank branch and a Schuler's Books and Music store were also located on the main floor. (Courtesy Michael Hauser.)

Three

THE WURZBURG COMPANY

WURZBURG'S LOWER MONROE AVENUE STORE, 1920S. The company was founded as a dry goods store in 1872 by Frederick W. Wurzburg. After occupying several buildings on Monroe Avenue, the growing retailer built a six-story emporium at 220 Monroe Avenue that opened in 1913. With additions in 1919 and 1926, Wurzburg's now encompassed 194,257 square feet, featured 109 departments, and employed 600 associates. (Courtesy Collections of the Grand Rapids Public Museum.)

ANNIVERSARY SALE PARADE, 1934. Wurzburg's store on Lower Monroe Avenue was the first retailer in town to have escalators and cash registers with drawers for each sales associate. Frederick Wurzburg retired in 1906 and passed on at age 90 in 1924. His sons William and Edmund ran the store until it was purchased by Sperry and Hutchinson (S&H Green Stamps) in 1936. This location closed in 1949, when Wurzburg's moved to Upper Monroe Avenue, but it reopened as a Trading Center in 1955. The company sold the building in 1961 to the city for the downtown urban renewal project. (Courtesy Collections of the Grand Rapids Public Museum.)

BOND STREET DOCK, 1920S. Wurzburg's early delivery methods were unique. When a guest wanted a package delivered, their name and address were written on the parcel, and it was delivered on a pushcart by associates of the store who lived in the direction the package was going. In later years, horse-drawn carriages were introduced. Streamlined trucks and vans were the third step in Wurzburg's delivery cavalcade. (Courtesy Collections of the Grand Rapids Public Museum.)

FOOD DIVISION AT WURZBURG'S, 1930S. Dining was a tradition at Wurzburg's since the early days on Lower Monroe Avenue, seen here. With the move to Monroe and Ottawa Avenues, the store expanded its offerings to include a downstairs snack bar, the Fountain Lunch Room for counter service, and the upscale Campau Room, which seated 125. Additionally, there were the epicure shop and the bakery, which stocked imported and domestic delicacies. (Courtesy Collections of the Grand Rapids Public Museum.)

WURZBURG'S HOLIDAY BILLBOARD, 1940S. Wurzburg's utilized Santa Claus to its best advantage via billboards, print media, direct mail, and radio. This billboard depicts Santa in front of the store on Lower Monroe Avenue. Following the Wurzburg Santa Claus Parade in 1919, Santa arrived at the store after circling the city for several hours in an airplane, dropping toys for boys and girls. (Courtesy Michael Hauser.)

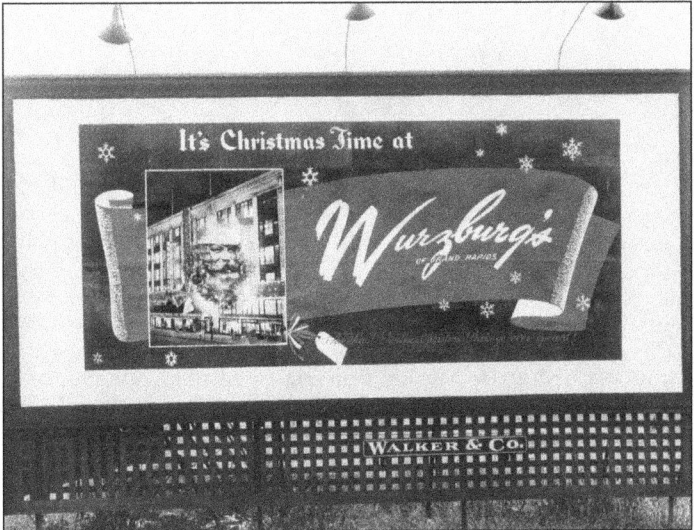

for 75 Years
IN GRAND RAPIDS
IT HAS BEEN
Wurzburg's

In Grand Rapids there is a white-haired lady who vividly recalls the Christmas of 1872. Her eyes still shine like diamonds when remembering she wore her first real party dress, made by her mother from wonderful bright red velvet yard goods from Wurzburg's.

Wurzburg's is a store that has brought happiness into the homes of Grand Rapids and throughout all of Western Michigan for seventy-five years.

1947 is its Diamond Jubilee year. Even when it was a tiny half-a-store with only yard goods, notions and groceries, the choice and beauty of Wurzburg's cottons, velvets, and satins brought the fashionable ladies in their carriages; and small boys whirled up on their high-wheeled bikes to fetch the newest delicacies for their mothers.

For Grand Rapids has always been a city of homes, of skilled craftsmen and cultured families who love comfortable, gracious living.

For them, with service, style and quality, Wurzburg has progressively built to commanding leadership.

Its alert fashion departments, and inspirational home floors, present the newest and the finest from so many of the nation's best known resources, coast-to-coast.

Wurzburg for its 75th, Diamond Jubilee year is the recognized fashion and home center of Western Michigan. It is the store of famous names. This is Wurzburg of Grand Rapids.

EVEN BACK IN 1872 GRAND RAPIDS WAS KNOWN AS A CITY OF HOMES. The Haldane homestead, now site of the Michigan Trust Company.

Wurzburg
OF GRAND RAPIDS   1872   1947
DIAMOND JUBILEE YEAR

75TH ANNIVERSARY MARKETING, 1947. For the diamond anniversary of the store, Wurzburg's commissioned artist Miriam Suleeba to paint various scenes of Grand Rapids that depicted art, industry, and commerce. An exhibit was installed in the store, and the paintings were also featured in advertisements and on a commemorative calendar. Scenes included Campau Square, the Pavilion at Reed's Lake, St. Mark's Episcopal Church, and the original Wurzburg store. (Courtesy Michael Hauser.)

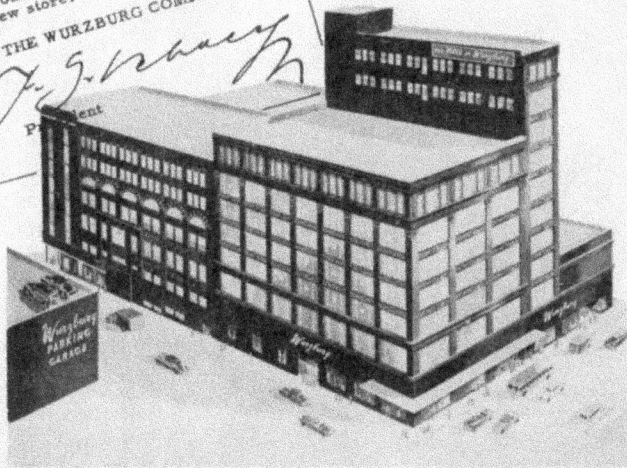

WURZBURG'S EMPLOYEE PUBLICATION, 1949. This special edition of *Around the Store* covered the store's big move to Upper Monroe Avenue. A special song—"Roll Up Monroe Street!"—was created for the move: "We'll roll up Monroe Street, let everyone hear the great news. We'll move to new quarters, with never a thought of the blues. Here comes more business, we're happy we're moving so soon! Yes, everyone will join us in singing, our gay move up tune!" (Courtesy Michael Hauser.)

ARTIST'S RENDERING OF RENOVATED BUILDING, 1949. Wurzburg's negotiated a 30.5-year lease in August 1949 on the former Herpolsheimer and Siegel store buildings and several surface parking lots on Louis Street. All of these properties were owned by the estate of the late William G. Herpolsheimer. Wurzburg's, with its increased volume, needed to seek larger quarters. (Courtesy Michael Hauser.)

PICTORIAL CUTAWAY DIRECTORY, 1951. The "Heart" campaign coincided with the store's move to 101 Monroe Avenue in 1951. Employees as well as guests were provided with red heart buttons to wear that declared: Wurzburg's . . . the store with you at heart!" These directories were sent to 150,000 of the store's guests. (Courtesy Michael Hauser.)

Monroe Ave. Looking West
Grand Rapids, Michigan

OUT WITH THE OLD AND IN WITH THE NEW, 1950S. The closing of the former Wurzburg's store at 220 Monroe Avenue and the move to the new store at 101 Monroe went smoothly. The move was accomplished between Saturday and Monday morning. Thanks to an aggressive marketing campaign, the store sold almost all of the merchandise at the old location. The opening ceremonies on Monday brought tremendous crowds, and sales for the first year in the new location hit $20 million. (Courtesy Michael Hauser.)

GRAND RAPIDS, MICHIGAN

NEW VERTICAL SIGN, 1961. Jane Wurzburg Bowen (granddaughter of the store's founder) pulled the remote control switch at the dedication ceremony to unveil this new signage in December 1961. The impressive, illuminated sign was 56 feet tall, stretching from the store's second floor to the sixth floor. (Courtesy Michael Hauser.)

EMPLOYEE HANDBOOK, 1950S. The Wurzburg's employee handbook, like those of other retailers, was filled with inspirational stories of the company's founding and detailed information on selling as well as nonselling functions. Additionally, there were explanations of the many employee perks, the group insurance and retirement plan, vacation days, sick pay, and retirement planning. (Courtesy Michael Hauser.)

YOUR GUIDE TO PLEASANT CHRISTMAS SHOPPING

Wurzburg OF GRAND RAPIDS

HOLIDAY SHOPPING GUIDE, 1960. Employees at Wurzburg's new location were ecstatic in their new home. The new store encompassed 293,007 square feet of selling space. There were 158 departments, 129 fitting rooms, custom-made fixtures from Grand Rapids Store Equipment, roomy escalators, and self-leveling, electronically controlled Otis elevators. The new store employed 1,000 associates. (Courtesy Michael Hauser.)

MONROE AVENUE EXTERIOR, 1956. To familiarize guests with the new store, Wurzburg's had hostesses attired in a specially designed uniform of Wurzburg green to act as concierges. Green telephones were located on each floor, connecting guests to the 10th-floor switchboard. The switchboard staff grew from 6 to 10 associates, trained to handle 40,000 calls a day. (Courtesy Grand Rapids History & Special Collections, Archives, Grand Rapids Public Library.)

SANTA PARADE AT CAMPAU SQUARE, 1950. Wurzburg's Santa Claus Parade began in 1919, commencing on the second Saturday in November, regardless of weather conditions. During the heyday of the parade in the 1960s, the lineup consisted of 29 balloons, 16 floats, nine bands, color guards, a drum-and-bugle corps, and clowns that traversed the two-mile route. Beginning in 1955, the parade was broadcast on WOOD TV (Grand Rapids), WKZO (Kalamazoo), and WWTV (Cadillac). (Courtesy Grand Rapids History & Special Collections Archives, Grand Rapids Public Library.)

WURZBURG'S SANTA CLAUS PARADE AT MONROE AND OTTAWA AVENUES, 1938. The parade was assisted by 500 Wurzburg's employees and 100 Boy Scouts. The company contracted with the Giant Balloon Company of Newark, New Jersey, for the balloons. The theme of each parade revolved around favorite storybook characters. Following the parade, Santa received a proclamation from the mayor, and then it was time to visit Santa and Mickey Mouse in Wurzburg's Toyland. (Courtesy Grand Rapids History & Special Collections, archives, Grand Rapids Public Library.)

SANTA CLAUS PHOTOGRAPH
PORTFOLIO, 1950. Santa has been
synonymous with Wurzburg's since
debuting in the toy department
in 1911, when the store was on
Lower Monroe Avenue. Most
Grand Rapidians would agree
that the "real" Santa lived on the
sixth floor at Wurzburg's. Neither
Toyland or the Christmas parade
would ever have been the same
without Ralph Weckenman, a
29-year employee and the store's
best-known Santa from 1945 to
1958. (Courtesy Michael Hauser.)

it's Christmastime at Wurzburg's

A PHOTOGRAPH WITH SANTA AT
WURZBURG'S, 1950s. Wurzburg's Santa
was featured on radio during the *Today
at Wurzburg's* program in the late
1950s on stations WOOD, WGRD,
WJEF, WFUR, and WLAV. In the
1960s, Santa had his own television
program on WOOD three days a week,
at 4:30 p.m., reading letters to Santa
on air. (Courtesy Michael Hauser.)

ROY ROGERS APPEARANCE, 1950. No visit to Grand Rapids by leading personalities of the day was complete without a visit to Wurzburg's. The largest crowds to gather at the store included those for visits from Liberace in 1954, and Lassie in 1958, when a crowd of 5,000 lined up to see television's wonder dog. Local cowboy personality Buck Barry and his horse, Thunder II, made their first public appearance in town at Wurzburg's in 1956. (Courtesy Grand Rapids History & Special Collections, Archives, Grand Rapids Public Library.)

OTTAWA AVENUE PARKING PAVILION, 1951. Wurzburg's constructed a multilevel, 500-space parking pavilion directly across the street from the Ottawa Avenue entrance to the store. A popular guest perk was the package-to-car service, whereby people could have the store deliver packages directly to their vehicle. At its peak, this garage handled 200,000 vehicles annually. (Courtesy Michael Hauser.)

HERE is the

Inside Story

of how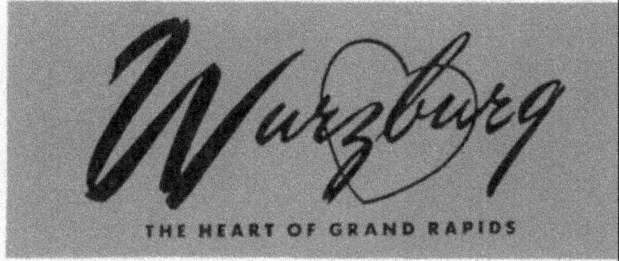

THE HEART OF GRAND RAPIDS

. . . is going to give more service to our customers

. . . with TWO HOURS MORE Shopping Time when the customers want it

. . . But with NO MORE WORKING TIME FOR YOU

HERE'S WHY

Wurzburg is Adding

FRIDAY NIGHT OPENINGS

STARTING FRIDAY, MAY 9

. . . and what it means *TO YOU*

EXTRA SHOPPING HOURS, 1952. As consumers began moving to the suburbs, retailers responded with evening store hours. Initially, Wurzburg's was open only two evenings a week until 9:00 p.m. By the 1960s, Wurzburg's stunned the business community by keeping its downtown store open each evening until 9:30 p.m. The store expanded the evening hours based on feedback from consultants and focus groups. (Courtesy Michael Hauser.)

WURZBURG'S PRESENTED WITH AWARD, 1956. The Distinguished Service Award of the American Dream Historical Society was presented to Wurzburg president Frederick Schoeck for public-service activities. Schoeck came to Wurzburg's from Germany in 1923 at the invitation of Edmund Wurzburg, the son of the founder. He started as an office boy before advancing to office manager, bookkeeper, and general manager. He became store president in 1944. (Courtesy Michael Hauser.)

FRIDAY, SEPTEMBER 23, 9:30 A.M. 'TIL 9 P.M. IS...

PRESIDENT'S DAY at *Wurzburg* OF GRAND RAPIDS

PRESIDENT'S DAY IS THE BIG DAY, the big day of extra, SUPER SAVINGS at Wurzburg's ANNIVERSARY SALE. Fred G. Schoeck, Wurzburg President, started at the store 37 years ago as office boy. He rose to the top, an example of the opportunity of THE AMERICAN WAY OF LIFE for those who work hard and know what the public wants.

WURZBURG CELEBRATES PRESIDENT'S DAY the way he knows you like best, with super savings for you. Every buyer has been planning and working for months to have for you EXTRA SAVINGS for President's Day. These are brand new items, never shown or advertised before during this Anniversary Sale. The biggest savings for the sale — for Friday, September 23, President's Day, 9:30 A.M. to 9:00 P.M.

FREE A BAG OF MICHIGAN *Flavorbest* APPLES TO THE FIRST 1,000! FIRST FLOOR AT ESCALATOR

S&H GREEN STAMPS

FREE ONE-HOUR PARKING, FRIDAY ONLY!
Park at any Downtown Parking lot — have this card validated at Wurzburg's S&H Green Stamp desk, 1st floor. Present it to the attendant for one hour's free parking. Wurzburg pays the charge.

Wurzburg 88th anniversary and it's GREAT Sale

PRESIDENT SCHOECK HAS A SALE, 1960. Part of the marketing strategy for the store's annual anniversary sale was to bolster the sale by combining it with an event such as President's Day. This was the final such event for Schoeck, who retired in 1961 following an illustrious career with Wurzburg's. His dynamic leadership brought the store to national prominence among the leading department store organizations. (Courtesy Michael Hauser.)

STAR GIFT PROMOTION, 1957. Wurzburg's holiday kickoff each year commenced in early November with a plethora of events that included the Santa Claus Parade, the employee holiday kickoff, the public House Warming open house, employee-family shopping days, and Star Gift promotions. With December came the men's club holiday-style shows and bazaars. (Courtesy Michael Hauser.)

HOLIDAY OPEN HOUSE, 1950s. One of the most anticipated events of the year for many guests was Wurzburg's House Warming. This was the evening when the store unveiled its animated display windows and interior and exterior holiday decor and lights, and children got a glimpse of the year's hottest toys and games while waiting to see Santa and Mickey Mouse and ride the merry-go-round. (Courtesy Michael Hauser.)

MUSIC TO THE EARS, 1950s. Besides the voices of the harmonious Wurzburg's Choir, guests were treated to sounds of the cathedral chimes, located on the roof of the store, that would play throughout the day. Another must for young ones was to ride the elevators. Wurzburg's was the first retailer in town to install "talking elevators" in the early 1960s. Upon boarding a car, a polite voice chimed in, "Welcome to Wurzburg's. Please touch button for your floor and step back. Going up!" (Courtesy Michael Hauser.)

HOLIDAY OPEN HOUSE, 1950s. What would an open house be without complimentary food and beverage? The Wurzburg's candy girls took care of those folks craving a sugar fix by dispensing trays of delicious holiday candies. For those desiring a quiet break, punch and cookies were served by candlelight in the store's Campau Room restaurant. (Courtesy Michael Hauser.)

HOLIDAY OPEN HOUSE, 1950s. During the 1950s, the store's holiday slogans included "Christmas isn't Christmas without a day at Wurzburg's" and "Wurzburg's . . . everybody's Christmas store!" During the early 1960s, the theme was "there's magic in a gift from Wurzburg's!" In 1963, the store debuted a massive, seven-story, illuminated Christmas tree on the Monroe Avenue exterior of the building, and the holiday slogan became "Behind the great tree . . . where the fun of Christmas begins!" (Courtesy Michael Hauser.)

A Holiday Time-Saver, 1950s. Yet another Wurzburg holiday tradition to assist guests was "Merrie Carol," the store's personal shopper program. Each department had an associate wearing a Christmas wreath badge and ribbon identifying themselves as a "Merrie Carol." This associate could assist with specific gift selections or shop and package a customer's complete gift list. (Courtesy Michael Hauser.)

Wurzburg's Choir, 1959. A time-honored holiday tradition of the House Warming evening was listening to the wonderful Wurzburg's Chorus, strolling musicians who also sang on the store's escalators. Additionally, guests were entertained by local radio personalities, an organist, an accordionist, and strolling troubadours. (Courtesy Michael Hauser.)

VAN HEUSEN SUPERBA TIES, 1950s. A lifesaver for men, these dress ties, introduced in the early 1950s, were made from Dacron, a new synthetic polyester fabric developed by DuPont. The beauty of Dacron was that it was machine washable, durable, stain resistant, and it required no pressing. (Courtesy Michael Hauser.)

MEN'S ROMEO SLIPPERS, 1950s. The quality and durability of these men's slippers is legendary. Romeo slippers were first introduced in the 1930s. The soft, wool fibers of natural fleece are breathable and act as a natural insulator to keep feet warm, dry, and comfortable. (Courtesy Michael Hauser.)

67

GIFT-BOXED IRISH LINEN HANDKERCHIEFS, 1950s. Hand-rolled linen handkerchiefs have been a tradition with gentlemen for decades. They are long lasting, and once laundered are quite soft. Linen is the original handkerchief fiber. Wurzburg's also offered personal embroidered initials, available with purchase. (Courtesy Michael Hauser.)

YARDLEY OF LONDON BOXED FRAGRANCE SETS, 1950s. Yardley, one of the world's oldest fragrance companies, has been trusted by guests for generations. Yardley soaps were introduced to American shoppers in 1879, and fragrances debuted in 1921. Yardley's signature fragrance was English Lavender, a scent that combined lavender leaves, neroli, and dry sage with a heart of lavender oil and geranium. (Courtesy Michael Hauser.)

CORO COSTUME JEWELRY
DISPLAY, 1950s. The sign
on the counter in the
accessories department is
promoting an appearance
from a representative of
Coro Jewelry. Coro was
one of the world's largest
jewelry-manufacturing
concerns for almost 75
years. The company
was best known for its
delicate yet sturdy floral
designs and romantic
brooches, many of
which are collectibles
today. (Courtesy
Michael Hauser.)

TRIM THE HOME SHOP, 1950s. The trim-a-tree department at Wurzburg's debuted on the fifth
floor each October, along with the personalized Christmas card department. One of the best
sellers throughout the 1940s and 1950s was Shiny-Brite holiday ornaments, which were affordable,
nicely packaged, and made in America. (Courtesy Michael Hauser.)

LINING UP FOR SANTA, 1959. For business associates who did not have the patience to shop in the store, Wurzburg's Gift Bar was set up each holiday season at the nearby Peninsular Club. Additionally, Wurzburg's produced holiday-style shows for the Lions Club, the Optimist Club, the Knights of the Round Table, the American Business Club, the Exchange Club, the Advertising Club, and the Sales Executives Club, all hosted at downtown hotels. (Courtesy Michael Hauser.)

WAITING FOR MICKEY, 1959. Another highlight of the holiday season at Wurzburg's was the annual Orphans Holiday Shopping Day, sponsored by the Grand Rapids Junior Chamber of Commerce each November. Employees and chamber members assisted underprivileged children as they shopped for themselves and loved ones that might not be able to receive holiday gifts. (Courtesy Michael Hauser.)

GALAXY OF GAMES IN TOYLAND, 1950S. The question of how to possibly pay for everything on Santa's gift list was answered in the 1950s and 1960s by Wurzburg's Christmas Club. One could purchase holiday gifts in October and not worry about paying for them until February of the following year. (Courtesy Michael Hauser.)

HOLIDAY GRIDLOCK ON THE SIXTH FLOOR, 1959. Another unique treat for children while shopping at Wurzburg's was the Penny Candy Shop. Youngsters were on their honor to drop pennies into large glass jars after making their purchase. (Courtesy Michael Hauser.)

AN EVEN LARGER TOYLAND OPENS, 1965. Wurzburg's was light-years ahead of today's pop-up shops when it first opened the Toyland of More in 1955. The company leased 12,000 square feet of space on three floors of a building adjacent to the main store. It was hailed as Michigan's largest toy store under one roof. (Courtesy Michael Hauser.)

AN EVER-EXPANDING TOYLAND, 1960s. The first floor featured dolls, costumes, trains, electronic toys, stuffed animals, and infant and educational toys and games. The second floor contained wheeled goods, furniture, gym sets, large games, a hobby shop, skis, sleds, and toboggans. The third floor housed a penny arcade, amusement rides, and a theater featuring daily live entertainment. (Courtesy Michael Hauser.)

72

ANIMATED HOLIDAY ANGEL WINDOW, 1950S. Wurzburg's animated holiday windows are legendary. Typically, there were five scenes, featuring 30 to 50 figures, that occupied three large Monroe Avenue display windows. The scenes took several months to construct in the store's warehouse, fit to the exact dimensions of the display window. Three semi-tractor trailers would then transport the displays to the downtown store. (Courtesy Michael Hauser.)

MELODIES IN THE WOODS, 1960. The tagline for this harmonious window display reads, "Christmas concert in the woods gives voice to song and merry moods. Holding hands and full of glee, they dance around the Christmas tree!" (Courtesy Michael Hauser.)

PRE-SANTA BEAR, 1960. The tagline for this busy "Christmas in the Forest" window display reads, "The forest creatures feel the spell of yuletide joy. They sing Noel. They keep in tune with tiny paws. A chubby bear plays Santa Claus." (Courtesy Michael Hauser.)

WOODLAND BABIES IN THE SNOW, 1960. The tagline for this "Christmas in the Forest" window display reads, "Woodland babies like the fare. Crisp and snowflaked winter air. Flashing by on tiny sleds. With thoughts of Christmas in their heads." (Courtesy Michael Hauser.)

STORYBOARD FOR HOLIDAY TELEVISION COMMERCIAL, 1960s. This heartwarming television commercial captured the magic of a trip to Wurzburg's during the holiday season with a mother and daughter. These scenes, filmed at the downtown store, included the main floor's holiday decor, Toyland, the animated holiday windows, and the store's signature green-and-yellow shopping bag. (Courtesy Michael Hauser.)

S&H GREEN STAMPS, 1953. Sperry and Hutchinson, longtime owners of Wurzburg's, opened a new S&H Green Stamp Redemption Center on the sixth floor in 1953, doubling the space of the former redemption center. This was the largest center of its kind in Michigan, with over 1,500 items and self-selection. (Courtesy Michael Hauser.)

ALIANZA PRODUCT
PROMOTION, 1967.
This promotion
was produced in
cooperation with the
Alliance for Progress
program, which was
initiated by Pres. John
F. Kennedy. The goal
of this program was
to establish a better
working relationship
between the United
States and Latin
America. (Courtesy
Michael Hauser.)

IMPORT SPECTACULAR, 1967. This departmental display on the sixth floor included handmade gifts from Bolivia, Columbia, Ecuador, and Peru. The Alliance for Progress program ended up being a multibillion-dollar program that endorsed land reform, free trade between Latin American countries, educational improvements, and the continued promotion of democracy. (Courtesy Michael Hauser.)

This two-week extravaganza began in 1955, highlighting imported merchandise from over two dozen countries. Wurzburg president Schoeck and the store buyers scheduled treks to Europe to make special purchases for this once-a-year special event. This window display features continental knits from Switzerland. (Courtesy Michael Hauser.)

EUROPEAN GIFTS, 1950s. Wurzburg's prided itself that store president Frederick Schoeck and his staff personally selected unusual collectors' items for the annual Import Fair. Large entry signs hailed, "Walk through our entrance into Europe!" These events allowed guests to obtain a taste of the more unique offerings from around the world. (Courtesy Michael Hauser.)

BRITISH AND GERMAN WARES, 1950S. Royal Doulton has produced tableware and collectibles in Great Britain dating back to 1815. The company is known not only for high-quality bone china, but also for stoneware, ceramics, figurines, vases, and decorative pieces. Rosenthal, founded over 125 years ago in Germany, is known for sophisticated, contemporary design and art in porcelain and glass. (Courtesy Michael Hauser.)

EUROPEAN CASUAL KNITS, 1950S. Throughout the 1950s, the store used the tagline, "the Wurzburg look . . . always the look of fashion!" The retailer had its own live television program, *The World of Fashion*, each Thursday that featured fashion tips, guest celebrities, models, and door prizes. It was broadcast over WOOD (Grand Rapids), WKZO (Kalamazoo), and WPBN (Traverse City). (Courtesy Michael Hauser.)

EUROPEAN ACCESSORIES, 1950s. Wurzburg's glitzy French Room on the second floor featured fashions and millinery from world-famous designers. Evan Picone custom-tailored coordinates were introduced in 1957. The store also had a Charles of the Ritz powder-blending salon. (Courtesy Michael Hauser.)

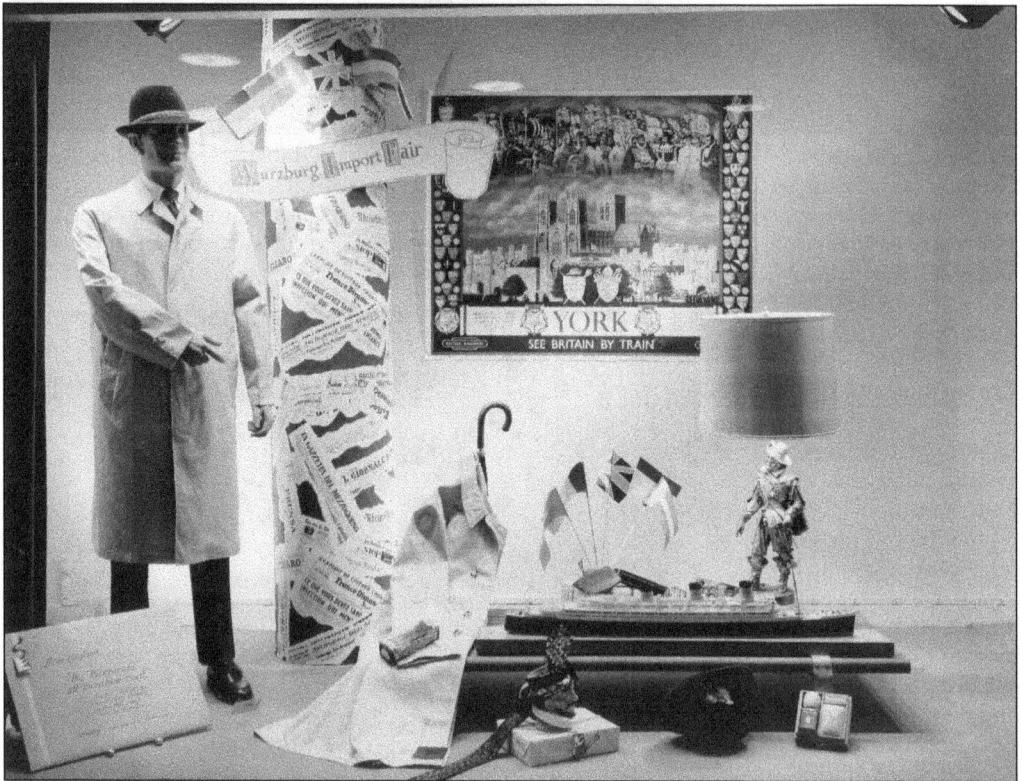

ENGLISH ALL-WEATHER COATS, 1950s. One of the best imports from Great Britain, the Harrington jacket from Baracuta, also known as the G9 jacket, debuted in 1938. The brand's popularity skyrocketed when Elvis Presley wore this jacket in the 1958 film *King Creole*. The jacket evolved from a short raincoat to a golf jacket, hence the G9 moniker. (Courtesy Michael Hauser.)

BACK TO SCHOOL PROMOTIONS, 1960S. In the 1940s and 1950s, the Collegienne Shop was "the place to shop." In the 1960s, the store had Modelette and Sub Deb modeling clubs with an in-store advisor for students. The high school and college advisory board students presented style shows, both in the store and at area schools, promoting the store's Young Michigan Shop. (Courtesy Michael Hauser.)

AUDITORIUM EXTRAVAGANZAS, 1960S. The store's sixth-floor auditorium became a virtual civic center unto itself through the years. This room was equipped for radio and television broadcasts, featured a stage, and could seat 275 guests. Through the years, it hosted fashion shows, art shows, cooking classes, sewing classes, lectures, demonstrations, teen dances, and appearances by authors and radio and television personalities. (Courtesy Michael Hauser.)

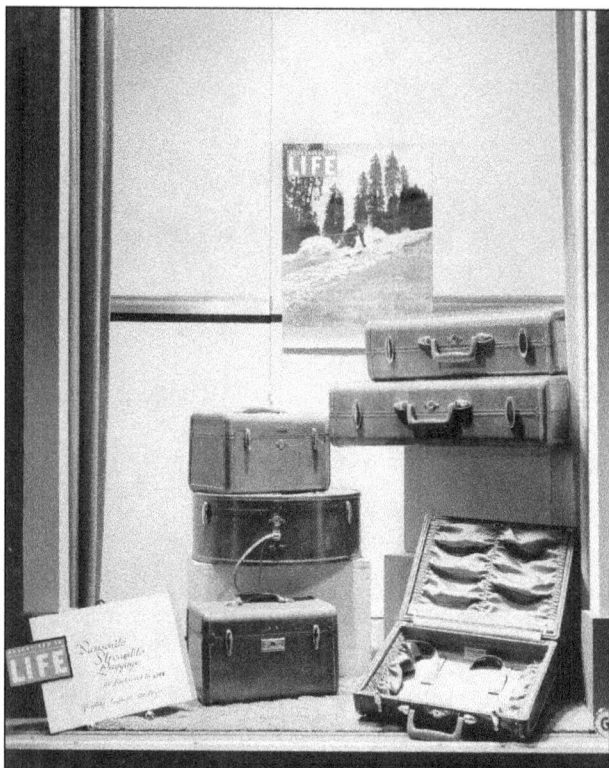

SAMSONITE LUGGAGE WINDOW DISPLAY, 1950s. Streamlite luggage was introduced in 1938 and became an immediate best seller. This luggage was scuff resistant, had an eye-catching shape, a lifetime-guaranteed handle, and precision-seal construction, which insured a perfect fit and no dust. (Courtesy Michael Hauser.)

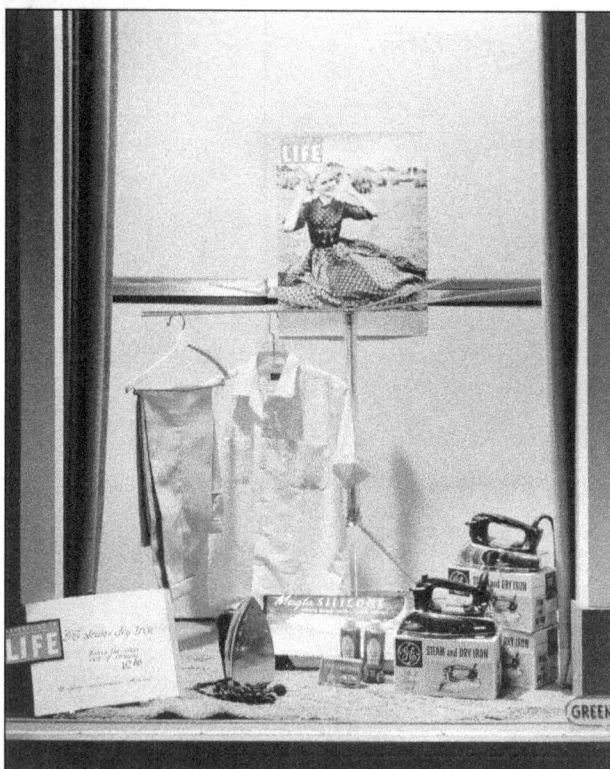

GE STEAM AND DRY IRON WINDOW DISPLAY, 1950s. When General Electric introduced this new iron in 1953, it was marketed as two irons in one. It could be used as a steam iron: pressing like a tailor, created instant steam, and did not require sprinkling. Or it could function as a dry iron: ideal for heavy cottons and linens, lighter in weight, and prevented scorching. (Courtesy Michael Hauser.)

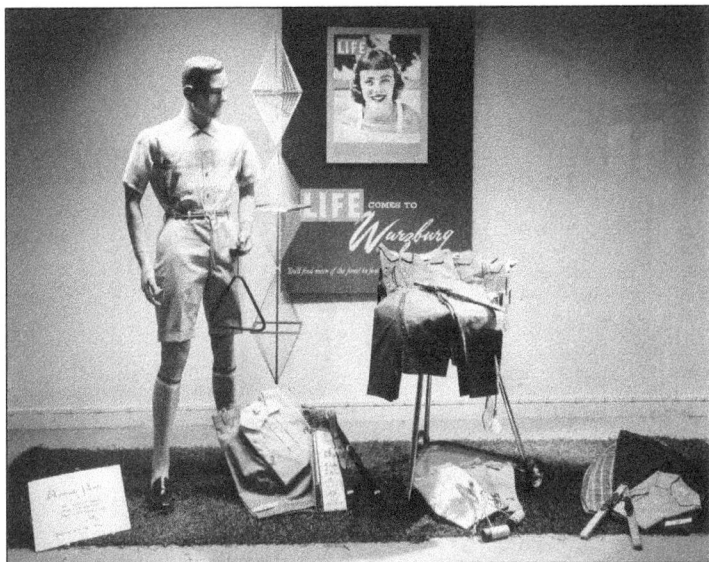

BERMUDA SHORTS
WINDOW DISPLAY, 1950S.
The English introduced
Bermuda shorts to the
people of Bermuda over
100 years ago. The British
army needed a tropical
uniform for the warmest
of the colonies, and
this was the solution.
Businessmen adopted
the short trousers in
the 1920s. Through the
years, the design has
been improved, and
more vibrant colors
and designs have been
introduced. (Courtesy
Michael Hauser.)

VAN HEUSEN WASH-AND-WEAR WINDOW DISPLAY, 1950S. In 1952, "wash-and-wear" was used to promote a new blend of cotton and acrylic. Commercial production of polyester fiber changed the wash-and-wear novelty into a revolution in textile product performance. By the 1960s and 1970s, clotheslines were replaced by electric dryers, and the wash-and-wear garments they dried emerged wrinkle free. (Courtesy Michael Hauser.)

ROBIN HOOD SHOES WINDOW DISPLAY, 1950S. Robin Hood Shoes was a popular line of children's shoes in the 1950s and 1960s, distributed by the Brown Shoe Company. The company promoted the line as "good for children's feet" and "good for parents' pocketbooks." (Courtesy Michael Hauser.)

JANTZEN SPORTSWEAR WINDOW DISPLAY, 1950S. Jantzen is one of the oldest and most-recognizable brand names for men's and women's sportswear. Back in the 1950s, it became the first apparel company to sponsor athletes and to utilize them in product endorsements. The company also incorporated Hollywood celebrities and public-awareness events into its marketing campaigns. (Courtesy Michael Hauser.)

If you have a credit card.....

from Diners' Club, Oil Companies or American Express

you can say "Charge it" at.....

Wurzburg
OF GRAND RAPIDS

Yes, it's so easy to say "Charge it" for
anything you select at Wurzburg! It's just
this simple: all you have to do is stop in
at Wurzburg's Credit Office, Fifth Floor, and
present your Diners' Club, Oil Company or
American Express credit card and your account
will be opened for you in a jiffy! You'll enjoy
shopping at Wurzburg, Grand Rapids' largest and
finest Department Store. Choose from Wurzburg's
large selections of merchandise bearing nationally
advertised, famous labels....fashions for yourself
and family....furniture and accessories for your
home.... exciting gifts, that will be beautifully
gift wrapped for you. Visit Wurzburg while you
are in Grand Rapids and enjoy the convenience of
"charging" your purchases!

Phone GL 9-5100

the

store of

famous

names

"CHARGE IT," 1960. This advertisement was geared toward conventioneers and visitors to Grand Rapids. At its peak in 1967, Wurzburg's had 86,000 charge customers. In 1969, the company was sold to John Butler, owner of Detroit's Demery's Department Stores, and the once-proud company began a gradual slide into oblivion. The downtown store closed in 1971, and by 1977 all branches were closed. (Courtesy Michael Hauser.)

DIRECT MAIL CAMPAIGNS, 1969. Wurzburg's was a pioneer with direct mail and brochures targeted to specific guests. Many remember the Mighty March Sale, the anniversary sale, Buy Days, and Women's Day. Several times in the 1950s and 1960s, Wurzburg's was selected by the Brand Names Foundation as the Retail Store of the Year in a nationwide competition. The store also received countless awards for its striking advertising campaign. (Courtesy Michael Hauser.)

Four

SPECIALTY RETAILERS

JACOBSON'S, 1940S. Jacobson's opened its first Grand Rapids specialty department store in 1943 on two floors of the north wing of what was then the Pantlind Hotel (today's Amway Grand Plaza Hotel). This space had previously been leased to the US Army for World War II efforts. (Courtesy Ella Sharp Museum-Jackson, Michigan.)

MAKING DO IN TIGHT SPACES, 1940s. Following World War II, when restrictions were lifted on building materials, Jacobson's completely renovated the first floor of the Pantlind store and added an I. Miller shoe salon. The retailer's customer service credo read: "As you know, there are such important values to be complemented in selective meticulous personal adornment. And we thoroughly subscribe to serve you!" (Courtesy Ella Sharp Museum-Jackson, Michigan.)

POWDER SALON AT JACOBSON'S, 1940s. Elegant wallpaper from the renowned F. Schumacher & Company was selected for the renovation of the shoe department, and rich draperies from the Grand Rapids Art Museum were purchased for the accessory departments and several lounges. (Courtesy Ella Sharp Museum-Jackson, Michigan.)

PRE-JACOBSON'S WATSON BUILDING, c. 1930. By the early 1950s, Jacobson's growth necessitated larger quarters, so the company leased the former Watson Building at Fulton and Sheldon Streets and provided it with a complete makeover. This renovation was hailed as "a dramatic symbol of Jacobson's continued acceptance in Grand Rapids!" (Courtesy Ella Sharp Museum-Jackson, Michigan.)

JACOBSON'S SOPHISTICATED NEW LOCATION OPENS, 1954. "The store of tomorrow" opened on August 11, 1954. This new location encompassed 36,000 square feet of space on the main and second floors and allowed the company to add a complete children's department and a men's furnishings department. The frontage on both Fulton and Sheldon Streets featured 15 large, well-lit display windows. (Courtesy Ella Sharp Museum-Jackson, Michigan.)

89

SHOE AND HANDBAG SALON, 1950s. The 1970s brought additional growth to the downtown store. In 1972, the company added a parking lot on the east side of the building. In 1973, Jacobson's added 35,000 square feet of selling space on the lower level for bridal merchandise, furs, china, gifts, stationery, draperies, and seasonal goods. The total combined amount of selling space now encompassed 70,000 square feet. (Courtesy Ella Sharp Museum-Jackson, Michigan.)

SWEATERS AND BLOUSES, 1950s. Competition and the reluctance of guests to travel downtown were cited as reasons for closing the downtown store in January 1978. In an unusual circumstance, virtually all of the employees were retained and transferred to the company's Wealthy Street store in East Grand Rapids. (Courtesy Ella Sharp Museum-Jackson, Michigan.)

EXTERIOR OF MAY'S, 1946. German immigrant Abraham May founded his store in 1883 at Monroe Avenue and Lyon Street. Originally called "the Giant," the company name was later changed to A. May & Sons when Abraham's children joined the firm. The store remained in the family until 1967, when it was purchased by Botany Industries. Norman Talmo, a former Botany executive, purchased the store in 1972. (Courtesy Grand Rapids History & Special Collections, Archives, Grand Rapids Public Library.)

LYON STREET WINDOWS AT MAY'S, 1953. May's enjoyed more window-display space than any other retailer downtown. One of the most-complete men's and boy's stores in West Michigan, it lived up to its slogan as "Grand Rapids' busiest clothier!" (Courtesy Collections of the Grand Rapids Public Museum.)

MAY'S DISPLAY FOR HARDIWEAVE SUITS, 1930S. In 1933, May's expanded its dress-shirt department and aggressively promoted monogramming. During this time, the store was hand embroidering 2,700 initials a month, and 23 associates were employed in the monogramming department. A semiannual Dollar Days event was also added to the store's promotional calendar in 1938. (Courtesy Collections of the Grand Rapids Public Museum.)

INTERACTIVE INTERIOR DISPLAY AT MAY'S, 1950S. By 1953, renovations to the store were in order. The first floor was updated, indirect lighting and rich wood trims were added, walls and ceilings were replastered, new exterior doors were installed, and entranceways were remodeled. Additionally, the boys' department was expanded, new lines were added to shoes, and a custom shop for made-to-measure merchandise was added. (Courtesy Collections of the Grand Rapids Public Museum.)

ACRES OF DRESS SHIRTS, 1930S. In 1954, a custom shop was introduced, offering an exceptional selection of imported and domestic woolens for suits, outer coats, sport coats, and slacks. Another phase of renovations was undertaken in 1969 that included new carpeting, new heating and cooling, upgraded offices, a new lower-level selling floor, and a complete face-lift to the exterior. (Courtesy Collections of the Grand Rapids Public Museum.)

WHEN MEN WORE DRESS HATS, 1920S. Knox Hats were the top of the line for haberdashery. They were worn by every American president until John F. Kennedy. The company ceased production in the 1960s, as the demand for hats decreased, and hats went from being a necessity to an optional wardrobe accessory. (Courtesy Collections of the Grand Rapids Public Museum.)

EVEN MORE DRESS HATS, 1920s. For decades, May's was the area's exclusive retailer for Hickey Freeman clothing, Burberry outerwear, Borsalino hats, and Michael's Stern evening wear. Even today, Hickey Freeman is known for authenticity, quality, elegance, and innovation. Additional and better names were added in the 1950s, including Hathaway shirts, Countess Mara neckwear, and Mark Cross gloves. (Courtesy Collections of the Grand Rapids Public Museum.)

MEN'S DRESS-SHIRT SPECIALISTS, 1951. In the early 1980s, May's added a Mayfair Shop next to the main store that exclusively sold women's apparel. The 1980s company slogan was, "It means more to be dressed by May's." However, guests were not shopping as often at May's, and the downtown store closed in 1986. The building was demolished for parking in 1988. (Courtesy Collections of the Grand Rapids Public Museum.)

MAY'S FAMOUS LEMON DAYS SALE, 1976. This sale was the largest promotional event of the year for May's. Guests would line up in the wee hours of the morning to claim a prominent spot in the queue to enter the store. Every bargain was from May's regular stock—either overstocks, odd sizes, or broken lots—and there were no special purchases. (Courtesy Collections of the Grand Rapids Public Museum.)

DISPLAY WINDOW AT HOUSEMAN'S FEATURING OUTERWEAR, 1922. Julius Houseman and his cousin Joseph immigrated to the United States from Germany and opened a clothing store on Monroe Avenue in 1852. Additional early partners in the business were Albert Alsberg, a Houseman cousin, and Abraham May, who eventually became a competitor with the establishment of what later became May's. (Courtesy Collections of the Grand Rapids Public Museum.)

FINEST CLOTHING STORE IN MICHIGAN

Largest Clothing Store in Western Michigan
HOUSEMAN & JONES, GRAND RAPIDS

TRADE POSTCARD FOR HOUSEMAN'S, 1913. Houseman's was known for its extensive selections of clothing, and in the 1880s it was described as having "probably the largest lines carried by any one house in the state!" The store moved three times through the years and eventually occupied its well-known location on Campau Square. In 1935, Houseman's promoted a radical new idea for that time: extended charge accounts, which extended the usual 30-day charge plan to 90 days. (Courtesy Michael Hauser.)

EXTERIOR OF HOUSEMAN'S, 1952. For many years, Houseman's, located at 140 Monroe Avenue, exclusively sold men's and boys' clothing. It was not until 1927 that the store began stocking women's apparel. The store was also known for its outstanding customer service, which included complimentary gift wrapping. Alas, because of changing consumer tastes, and with only the downtown location, the store closed in 1986. (Courtesy Grand Rapids History & Special Collections, Archives, Grand Rapids Public Library.)

FLORSHEIM SHOES, 1920s. Milton Florsheim founded his company in 1892 with a wish to produce high-quality men's dress shoes at a modest price. The company's growth escalated when he persuaded entrepreneurs to open their own Florsheim stores, such as this branch at 108 Monroe Avenue, which remained in business from the 1920s through the 1980s. (Courtesy Collections of the Grand Rapids Public Museum.)

FLORSHEIM SLEEK EXTERIOR REMODEL, 1930s. Florsheim outfitted generations of American men for school, work, and special occasions and arguably became the most famous brand in the shoe trade. The brand was positioned as "the aspirational shoe for the average guy!" By the 1950s, Florsheim had a 70-percent share of the men's dress-shoe market. (Courtesy Collections of the Grand Rapids Public Museum.)

EXTERIOR OF EHINGER SALON SHOES, 1959. Raymond Ehinger opened his shoe store on the main floor of this building at 2 Fulton Street East in the early 1950s. Ehinger gained a widespread reputation as a retailer specializing in narrow-width shoes. In the mid-1960s, the salon moved to 40 Monroe Avenue, and it relocated again in 1984 to the downtown City Centre mall. The company closed its doors in 1987. (Courtesy Grand Rapids History & Special Collections, Archives, Grand Rapids Public Library.)

FLEET OF DELIVERY TRUCKS FOR THE BOSTON STORE, 1929. The Boston Store was founded in 1885 on Campau Square by Charles Trankla, one of the most progressive merchants in the city at that time. What began as 30 feet of frontage evolved into six storefronts encompassing four floors, and by 1911 it was one of the largest retailers on Monroe Avenue. Employment grew from a modest crew of seven associates to nearly 300 employees. (Courtesy Collections of the Grand Rapids Public Museum.)

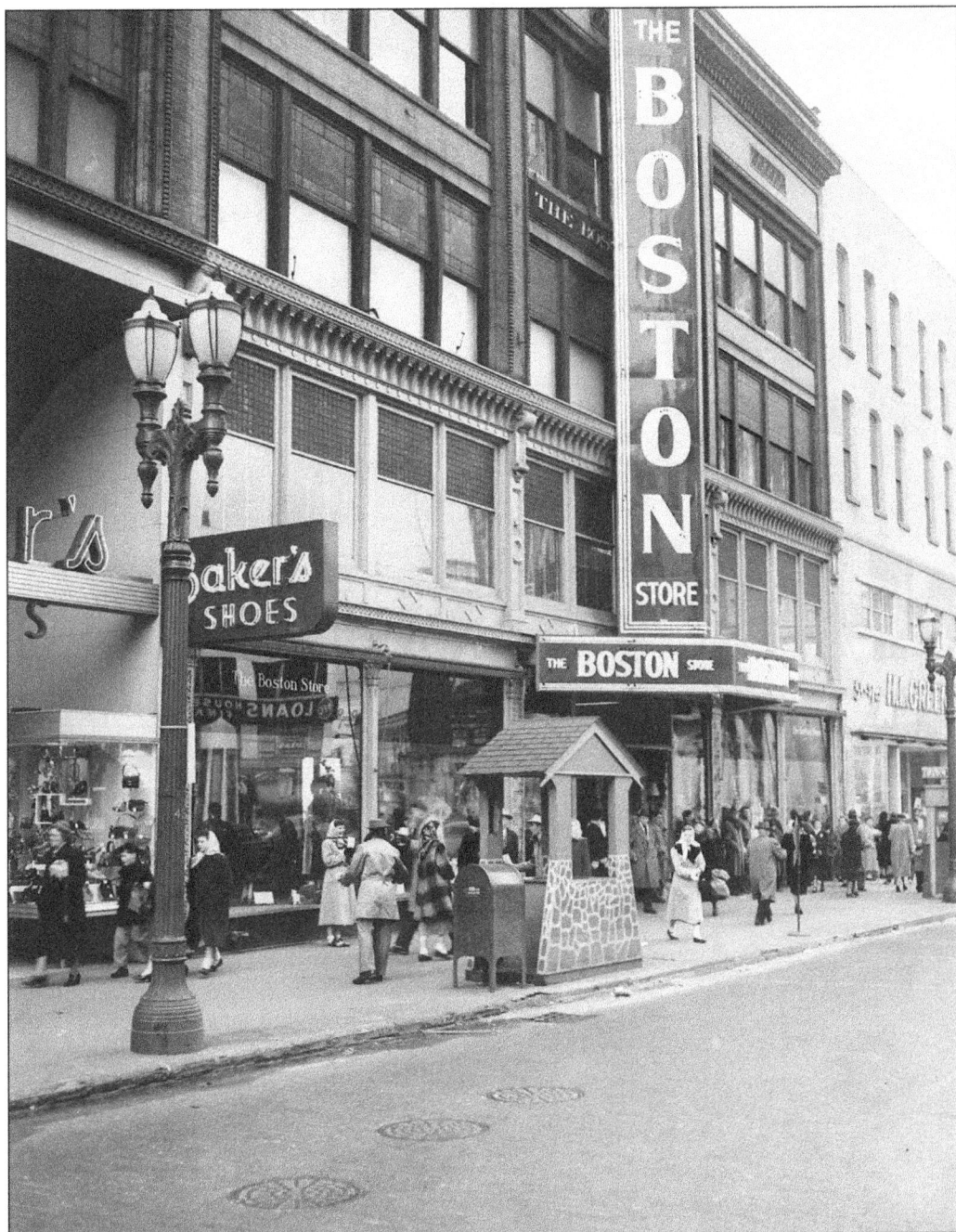

EXTERIOR OF THE BOSTON STORE, 1950. In the mid-1930s, the main floor of the Boston Store at 145 Monroe Avenue was renovated, aisles were widened, and modern elevators were installed. A moderately priced dress department was opened on the second floor, and the fourth floor was given a makeover for a complete home-furnishings department. The store slogan was "situated on the square . . . where your dollar buys more!" (Courtesy Grand Rapids History & Special Collections, Grand Rapids Public Library.)

PATTERN DEPARTMENT AT BOSTON STORE, 1915. Charles Trankla passed in 1930, and the store was then operated by his son-in-law C.R. Viele. Competition and changing consumer tastes drove the Boston Store into receivership in 1951. This space was then taken over by Darling Shops and an expansion of the neighboring H.L. Green Co. dime store. (Courtesy Collections of the Grand Rapids Public Museum.)

PECK'S DRUGS LUNCH COUNTER, 1940s. Peck's Drugs operated a branch at this Campau Square location from 1930 to 1967. Peck's slogan for decades was "save your time, and save your money!" Peck's was also one of the city's first all-night drugstores. (Courtesy Collections of the Grand Rapids Public Museum.)

EXTERIOR OF PECK'S DRUGS AT 34 MONROE AVENUE, 1965. John and Thomas Peck opened their drugstore in 1876 in this flatiron-styled structure at Monroe and Division Avenues. This "cut rate" drugstore was a Rexall affiliate for many years. In 1967, Peck's was purchased by Revco Drugs, who eliminated the Peck's name and closed this store in 1988, ending 112 years of continuous drugstore operation at this corner. (Courtesy Grand Rapids History & Special Collections, Archives, Grand Rapids Public Library.)

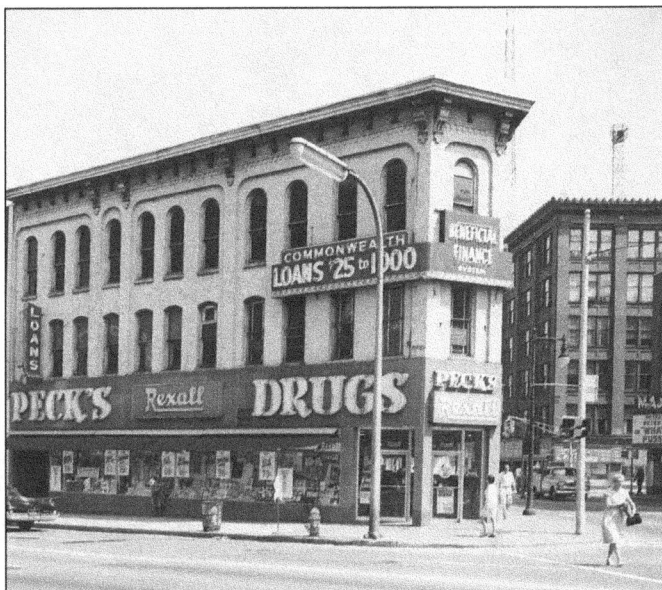

FOUNTAIN TERRACE AT PECK'S CAMPAU SQUARE, 1940s. Peck's was one of the earliest retailers in town to install a cash register. An advertisement in the 1892 *Grand Rapids Democrat* declared, "Peck's cash register: what does it do? A cheap, neat operation, durability, assured, and made by a business man for business men!" (Courtesy Collections of the Grand Rapids Public Museum.)

SODA FOUNTAIN AT PECK'S CAMPAU SQUARE, 1940S. At its peak in the 1940s, Peck's also had branch stores downtown at Monroe and Ionia Streets in the Morton House Hotel and at Monroe and Michigan Streets in the Rowe Hotel. The Campau Square branch closed in 1967 for the straightening of Monroe Avenue. (Courtesy Collections of the Grand Rapids Public Museum.)

DAANE AND WITTERS MARKET, 1957. The aisles of this foodie emporium at 2 Monroe Avenue featured gourmet treats enjoyed by generations from the mid-1930s through the mid-1960s. State College of Beauty occupied this space in the 1970s. A major fire severely damaged the space in 1980. Bob and Alecia Woodrick and Shirley Balk purchased the building in the mid-1990s and donated it to the Grand Rapids Children's Museum; it was renovated and reopened in 1997. (Courtesy Grand Rapids History & Special Collections, Archives, Grand Rapids Public Library.)

ART MODERNE SPLENDOR, 1947. The Hub was a popular men's store at 337 Monroe Avenue that featured upscale brands such as Kuppenheimer, a leading manufacturer of men's apparel. The store flourished from 1930 to 1960 but was doomed by the migration of retail to Upper Monroe Avenue and the impending urban renewal project of the 1960s that leveled this section of downtown. (Courtesy Grand Rapids History & Special Collections, Archives, Grand Rapids Public Library.)

YORK BAND INSTRUMENTS AT GRINNELL'S MUSIC, 1930s. Detroit-based Grinnell Brothers was West Michigan's music center for pianos, radios, sheet music, records, and band and orchestra instruments. The company manufactured pianos in Michigan for several decades. Its motto was "everything in the realm of music." (Courtesy Collections of the Grand Rapids Public Museum.)

SHEET MUSIC DEPARTMENT AT GRINNELL'S, 1930s. Grinnell's first location downtown was at 206 Monroe Avenue, which opened in the 1920s. The store then moved to 26 North Division Avenue, next to the Majestic Theatre, in the 1950s. When that lease ran out, the retailer returned to 121 Monroe and remained there until 1972. (Courtesy Collections of the Grand Rapids Public Museum.)

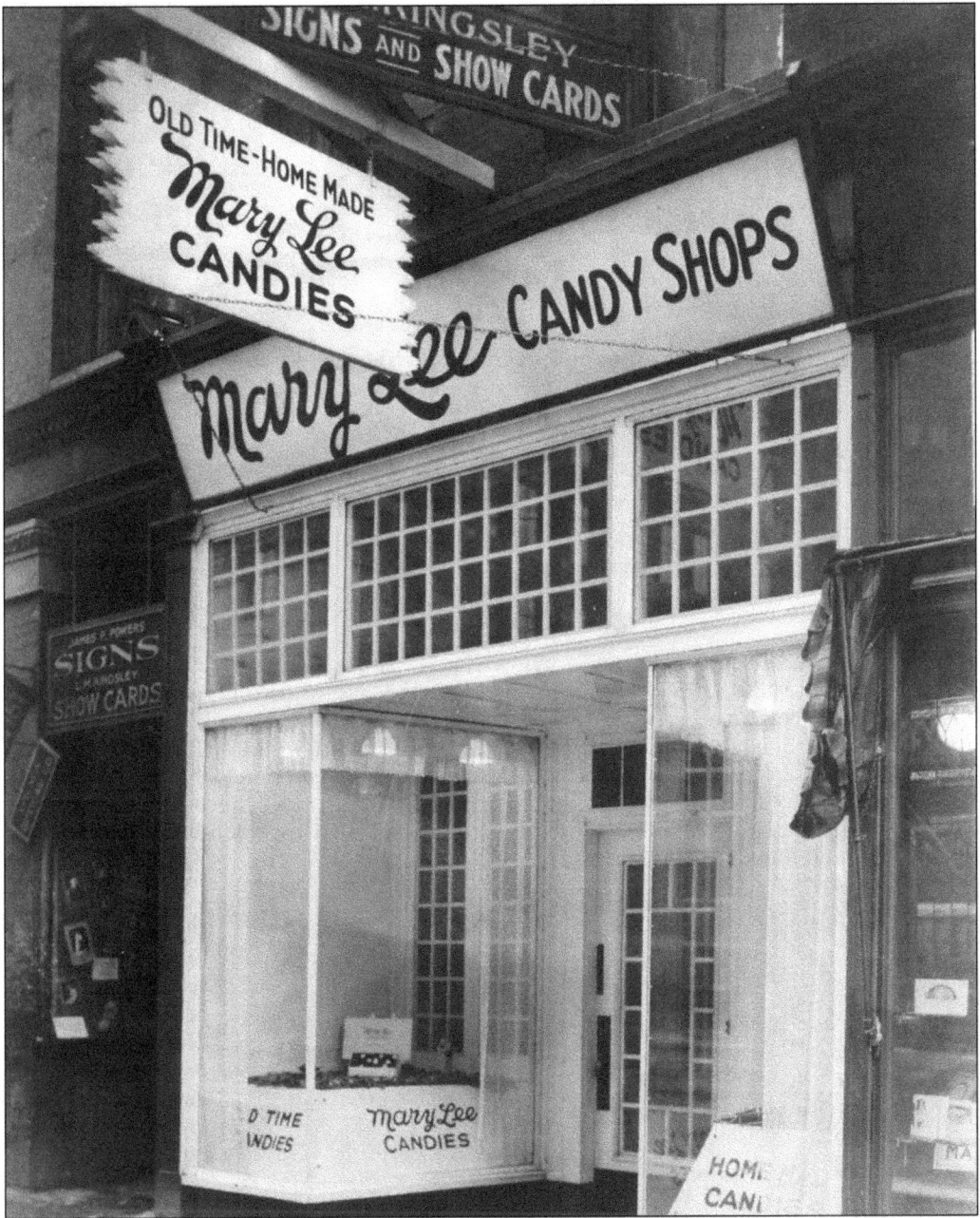

MARY LEE'S HOMEMADE CHOCOLATE, 1923. Mary Lee Candy was founded in Detroit in 1921 and shortly thereafter opened a downtown Grand Rapids store at 139 Pearl Street. Mary Lee products were sold in its company-owned stores, and by the mid-1920s it was the largest retailer of candy in Michigan. From the 1930s to the 1950s, the company operated a retail store at 81 Monroe Avenue and from 1950 to 1960 a full-service restaurant at 40 Monroe. (Courtesy Collections of the Grand Rapids Public Museum.)

FASHIONABLE SHOPPING, 1953. Theodore and Haseebie Gantos, two Lebanese immigrants, opened a lingerie and hosiery store at Monroe and Ottawa Avenues in 1932. The company was inherited by their four sons and, by the 1990s, grew to 115 stores in 24 states. The original location, seen here, closed in 1958 as the company concentrated on neighborhood locations. Gantos returned to downtown in 1967 at 39 Monroe and later moved into City Centre. The company was liquidated in 2000. (Courtesy Grand Rapids History & Special Collections, Archives, Grand Rapids Public Library.)

SHAW'S JEWELERS ON CAMPAU SQUARE, 1940S. Shaw's was a credit jeweler, guaranteeing the lowest cash prices on credit. From 1937 through 1975, the company called several locations along Monroe Avenue home, including McKay Tower, shown here. (Courtesy Collection of the Grand Rapids Public Museum.)

EXTERIOR OF BISHOP FURNITURE, 1928.
Bishop's was founded in 1895 as both
a manufacturer and retailer of home
furnishings. The Ionia Avenue building
depicted here was originally constructed
to house a Masonic Temple on the top
four floors and Grand Rapids Wholesale
Furniture on the lower three. Bishop's was
known as "the quality store" that shipped
merchandise anywhere. (Courtesy Collections
of the Grand Rapids Public Museum.)

TRUCK FROM BISHOP FURNITURE'S DELIVERY FLEET, 1920s. Despite the fact that Bishop's maintained
a large downtown store and opened branches elsewhere in Michigan, a great deal of the company's
sales came through its direct mail catalog. As downtown retailing declined, the store moved to
Michigan Street in 1981. Fierce competition forced the company to liquidate its assets in 2005.
(Courtesy Collections of the Grand Rapids Public Museum.)

EXTERIOR OF SEARS STORE AT 128 MONROE AVENUE, 1960s. Sears, Roebuck & Company operated a full-line department store on Monroe Avenue from 1929 to 1968. The store encompassed four floors in two buildings and was given a complete makeover in 1950. Additionally, Sears had an auto center at 242 Pearl Street, across from today's Amway Grand Plaza Hotel. (Courtesy Collections of the Grand Rapids Public Museum.)

SEARS DISPLAY WINDOW, 1930s. Sears was a pioneer in creating department stores that welcomed male guests by featuring various lines of hardware and building materials and allowing guests to select merchandise without the aid of a sales associate. Over the decades, Sears established many well-known national brands, including Kenmore, Craftsman, Coldspot, and DieHard. (Courtesy Collections of the Grand Raids Public Museum.)

HEADQUARTERS OF CONSUMERS POWER, 1941. Consumers Power Company maintained its regional offices and a showroom in the Powers Building on Pearl Street from 1919 to 1969. For decades, the bright lights of the four-story blade sign added to the excitement of the bustling Campau Square area. This structure and the adjoining Midtown Theatre were demolished in the late 1970s. (Courtesy Michael Hauser.)

SALES SHOWROOM OF CONSUMERS POWER, 1930. In the days prior to complete department stores, and later big-box retailers, guests visited the showrooms of Consumers Power Company to purchase their kitchen appliances, water heaters, washing machines, and electric appliances. To encourage guests to visit the showroom, Consumers provided free bus rides during its Open House Week. (Courtesy Collections of the Grand Rapids Public Museum.)

THOMPSON'S CAFETERIA, 136 MONROE AVENUE, 1960s. The Chicago-based John R. Thompson Company operated this popular lunch spot at 136 Monroe Avenue from the mid-1920s into the early 1970s, when it was then known as Clayton's Cafeteria. Thompson's had an advantageous location near Campau Square, sharing the block with Houseman's and Sears. (Courtesy Collections of the Grand Rapids Public Museum.)

INTERIOR OF THOMPSON'S CAFETERIA, 1940s. Thompson's was one of the earliest and largest cafeteria chains in the country. Its eclectic menu featured not only cafeteria staples, but also upscale sandwiches and salads. The company slogan was "eat Thompson's way, for a better day!" Many of its china and silver pieces are collectible items today. (Courtesy Collections of the Grand Rapids Public Museum.)

FANNY FARMER CANDIES, 1954. A Fanny Farmer outlet was located at the corner of Monroe and Ottawa Avenues from 1936 to 1995, making it one of the longest-operating retailers to call Monroe Avenue home. Only the finest ingredients were featured in its product offerings: real butter, fresh cream, fresh fruits, and premium nut meats. (Courtesy Grand Rapids History & Special Collections, Archives, Grand Rapids Public Library.)

SIEGEL'S WOMEN'S APPAREL, 1959. Siegel's, founded in the late 1890s, called several locations on Monroe Avenue home. The firm moved to 97-99 Monroe Avenue at Ottawa Avenue in 1940 and was acquired by Detroit-based Albert's in 1965, who kept this location open until 1975. Interestingly, the lower-level space with the marquee (Ottawa Avenue side) was home to a Meijer Supermarket from 1954 to 1958. The company felt this urban branch would benefit from retail and office foot traffic. (Courtesy Grand Rapids History & Special Collections, Archives, Grand Rapids Public Library.)

COYE'S TENTS AND AWNINGS, 1960. This business was founded by Albert Coye in 1855 on Lower Monroe Avenue. Its primary business was making sails, but the company diversified by producing tents and awnings. Charles Coye joined his father in 1882 and in 1911 incorporated the firm and moved into a four-story building at Louis and Campau Avenues, shown here. The firm moved to Grandville Avenue in 1981. (Courtesy Robert Goodrich.)

BASCH'S JEWELER'S, 1950S. Basch's was a Lower Monroe Avenue anchor from 1937 until 1960. The store was known for its diamonds, nationally advertised watches, radios, and movie equipment. Its catchy slogan was "you don't need cash with Basch!" The store was another victim of the downtown urban renewal program. (Courtesy Collections of the Grand Rapids Public Museum.)

MORTON MEN'S SHOP, 1940S. This small but classic men's store opened in 1930 on the main floor of the once fashionable Morton House Hotel at 80 Monroe Avenue. It flourished for over 40 years and closed in the early 1970s when the hotel was converted to affordable housing. Today, the hotel is being gutted for a new mixed-use development encompassing retail and residential functions that will open in 2015. (Courtesy Collections of the Grand Rapids Public Museum.)

KAMBER MEN'S CLOTHING, 1949. Kamber was a popular value men's clothing retailer. Its original location in 1940 was at 118 Monroe Avenue, prior to a move to 39 Monroe (pictured) in 1948. When Woolworth's decided to lease the entire main floor for a second Monroe store in 1959, Kamber moved to 192 Monroe. (Courtesy Grand Rapids History & Special Collections, Archives, Grand Rapids Public Library.)

PREUSSER JEWELERS, 1970s. Preusser Jewelers, the oldest jeweler in Michigan, was founded by William Preusser in 1850. The first location at Monroe and Ottawa Avenues was stocked with $10,000 worth of merchandise, and in 1880 it was one of the first retailers in town to have electric lights. The store made subsequent moves to locations on Monroe and Sheldon Streets and settled into the Kendall Building (pictured) in 1952. Preusser moved to 125 Ottawa Avenue in 1986. (Courtesy Robert Goodrich.)

FOX'S JEWELERS, 1920S. The Fox
Jewelry Company was founded
by Martin Fox in 1917 and was
initially located on Lower Monroe
Avenue before moving to a more
lucrative spot across from the
Pantlind Hotel (today's Amway
Grand Plaza Hotel). In 1949, the
company purchased the former
Peck Building (pictured) to be
closer to the major department
stores. Martin's son Tom joined
the company and worked there
during high school and college.
(Courtesy Collections of the
Grand Rapids Public Museum.)

LEGENDARY FOX BUILDING, 1997. A
trademark of the downtown store was a
35-foot-high vertical sign with a revolving
diamond. Fox's was a pioneer in local-
television advertising. Early advertisements
featured Martin purchasing diamonds
in Antwerp. Anyone who grew up
in town from the 1960s through the
1980s will remember the "Hi . . . I'm
Tom Fox" commercials. Tom sold the
business in 1997 to Fred Meyer Jewelers,
and the downtown store closed. The
entire building was renovated in 2012
and is home today to the City Flats
Hotel. (Courtesy Michael Hauser.)

HERKNER JEWELERS, 1925.
Perhaps the best-known jewelry store in town was founded in 1867 by Civil War colonel Joseph C. Herkner. Following his success on Lower Monroe Avenue, the firm moved to 114 Monroe Avenue in 1890 (shown here), and the company prospered until its departure for a suburban location in 2008. Note Groskopf's Luggage & Gifts to the right of Herkner (Courtesy Collections of the Grand Rapids Public Museum.)

WALK OVER SHOE STORE, 1929.
Walk Over Shoes, pictured here at 96 Monroe Avenue, was a product of the George E. Keith Company of Brockton, Massachusetts, and was for many years the premiere brand of men's footwear. Its specialties were the tailored business shoe and the classic buck. In later years, women's shoes and casual styles were introduced. (Courtesy Collections of the Grand Rapids Public Museum.)

Five

DIME STORES

KRESGE STORE NO. 59, 1929. Detroit-based S.S. Kresge Company replaced an older store with the two new buildings depicted in this postcard view of 135 Monroe Avenue. Selling floors included the lower level and the main floor, with offices and stockrooms on the second and third floors. Kresge was one of "the big three" of the dime store industry. (Courtesy Michael Hauser.)

CONSTRUCTION OF NEW KRESGE STORE, 1929. The original Kresge store, which opened in 1912, is seen here on the left, with Woolworth's in the background at Market Street. By the time the new building opened, most dime stores were forced to raise their prices to 25¢ and higher. Kresge's earliest presence on Monroe Avenue dates back to 1900 with a Kresge and Wilson dime store. (Courtesy Collections of the Grand Rapids Public Museum.)

ART DECO SPLENDOR, 1936. Kresge's new store featured white-and-gold terra-cotta with stylized neon and a handsome exterior clock. Store No. 59 was profitable for the company for many years, and its closing in 1977 ended the company's presence in downtown that had spanned over 75 years. The store was demolished for the straightening of Monroe Avenue. (Courtesy Collections of the Grand Rapids Public Museum.)

Holiday Hustle and Bustle at Kresge Korner, 1939. Monroe and Market Streets was nirvana for holiday shoppers as they trekked between Dime Store Row and downtown's multi-floored department store emporiums. Prior to the advent of discount stores, many folks purchased their holiday ornaments, trees, trim, ribbons, and wrapping paper at Kresge's. (Courtesy Grand Rapids History & Special Collections, Archives, Grand Rapids Public Library.)

Goodness Is Always in Season, 1936. A store display window devoted to bulk candy is difficult to imagine today. Kresge's popular candy department was always well stocked with a variety of delicious product. Customer favorites included rich chocolate crèmes, smooth velvet fudge, crisp peanut brittle, chewy kisses, jelly beans, lollipops, freshly roasted peanuts, and the ever-popular party mix. (Courtesy Collections of the Grand Rapids Public Museum.)

KRESGE'S *Specials* for TODAY

HOT OFF THE GRILL......AS YOU LIKE IT

1/4 LB. CHOPPED BEEF ON BUN, TOMATO SLICE, FRENCH FRIES AND SALAD	55¢
1/4 LB. HAMBURGER ON BUN, TOMATO SLICE, MUSTARD, RELISH, OR KETCHUP	39¢
CHEESEBURGER A HAMBURGER ON A HOT BUN WITH MELTED CHEESE AND SWEET RELISH	35¢
HAMBURGER WITH POTATO SALAD AND DILL PICKLE	40¢
GRILLED STEAK SANDWICH ON AN OPEN FACE BUN, TOMATO SLICE, FRENCH FRIES AND SALAD	60¢
GRILLED CHEESE WITH POTATO CHIPS	25¢
GRILLED HAM SANDWICH WITH FRENCH FRIES PICKLE CHIPS	50¢

FRENCH FRIED POTATOES 15¢
(LIBERAL PORTIONS)

GOOD CUP OF COFFEE 7¢
SERVED WITH PURE CREAM

DRINK Coca-Cola   To Avoid Mistakes Please Pay When Served   5¢

KRESGE LUNCHEONETTE MENU, 1940. Kresge's prided itself on serving hundreds of fresh, home-cooked meals daily to shoppers, the downtown office crowd, and conventioneers from the nearby Civic Auditorium and downtown hotels. All meals were served on real china with real silverware. (Courtesy Michael Hauser.)

The DINETTE

FOLD BACK HERE

THURSDAY, APRIL 21, 1977

VEGETABLE SOUP WITH SALTINES 35¢	#1 TODAY'S FEATURE MEAT LOAF LUNCHEON $1.39	"HOMEMADE" CHILI CON CARNE 65¢
GRILLED CHEESE SANDWICH POTATO CHIPS 58¢		FRESH STRAWBERRY SHORTCAKE WHIPPED TOPPING 65¢
HOT STACKED HAM SANDWICH 99¢	ADVERTISED SPECIAL #2 DELUXE HAMBURGER PLATE.....99¢ Hamburger Sandwich with Lettuce & Tomato Slice on a Hot Soft Bun Served with Golden Brown French Fries Choice of Condiments	CHOCOLATE PUDDING WHIPPED TOPPING 35¢
FRIED FISH SANDWICH 99¢	#3 HOT TURKEY SANDWICH......$1.19 Thin Sliced Roast Breast of Turkey White Bread Mashed Potatoes Rich Giblet Gravy Cranberry Sauce	JELLO WITH WHIPPED TOPPING 30¢
PATTY MELT SANDWICH 99¢	FOOD MANAGER SPECIAL #4	HOT APPLE DUMPLING W/SAUCE 59¢

it's the real thing Coca-Cola   To Avoid Mistakes Please Pay When Served

KRESGE DINETTE MENU, 1977. The final menu for the downtown Kresge store still featured all-time favorites such as grilled cheese and hot turkey sandwiches, hamburger platters, and a Coca-Cola. The popular snack bar near the Monroe Avenue entrance sold thousands of ham sandwiches and jumbo ice-cream sandwiches through the years. (Courtesy Michael Hauser.)

120

KRESGE'S FAMOUS LUNCHEONETTE, 1936. The ultimate dime store experience at Kresge's was to visit the luncheonette, which featured handsome marble counters, red swivel stools, stainless-steel napkin dispensers, and the whirl of the overhead paddle fans. Many guests have fond remembrances of popping a balloon for the chance to obtain a free banana split or hot-fudge sundae. (Courtesy Collections of the Grand Rapids Public Museum.)

FABRIC DEPARTMENT AT KRESGE'S, 1936. Back in the days when many women made their own clothing, a great deal of square footage in stores was devoted to fabric and fabric patterns. Simplicity Pattern Co. dominated the market for many years, presiding over a major education program that included fashion shows, educational books, and traveling sales representatives. (Courtesy Collections of the Grand Rapids Public Museum.)

WHAT A NICKEL WILL BUY, 1936. Kresge's featured just about everything one could imagine: baby needs, tools and electrical supplies, housewares, toys, window shades, notions, toiletries, clothing, cleaning supplies, and pets. One could even obtain passport photographs and get keys made. A favorite stop was also the photograph booth, which has made a comeback with today's younger generation. (Courtesy Collections of the Grand Rapids Public Museum.)

OPENING-DAY SPECIALS, 1936. Up until 1952, each department at Kresge's was staffed with a sales associate and a checkout register, as depicted in this image. To streamline operations and cut down on operational costs, central checkouts were installed. Despite the amount of merchandise packed into limited square footage, the store was well maintained. (Courtesy Collections of the Grand Rapids Public Museum.)

FRIEDMAN SPRINGS DRY GOODS, 1910s. This major retailer was established in 1854 by Daniel W. Spring. It was one of the first firms in town to have electric lights when they were illuminated in 1880. As the business grew, it moved to several locations on Monroe Avenue. By 1916, Spring merged with the M. Friedman Company. Hard times caused the business to close in 1930, and this space was then leased by the W.T. Grant Company. (Courtesy Collections of the Grand Rapids Public Museum.)

F&W GRAND STORE WINDOW, 1920S. This dime store was located at 157-159 Monroe Avenue, later the home of H.L. Green Company. At the time, sales of a dollar or more had to be approved by a manager or floorwalker, and money had to be registered before the goods were wrapped. Old-timers will remember this store for featuring the "original brown bobby," a greaseless doughnut that sold for 25¢ a dozen. (Courtesy Collections of the Grand Rapids Public Museum.)

H.L. Green Company Dime Store, 1952. Green's was a dime store chain founded in 1935 with the consolidation of the F&W Grand and Metropolitan Stores, both of whom had stores on Monroe Avenue. Green's expanded its Campau Square store in 1952 with a handsome Vitrolite facade, occupying part of the original Friedman Springs building. The company did not renew its lease and closed this store in 1964. (Courtesy Grand Rapids History & Special Collections, Archives, Grand Rapids Public Library.)

W.T. Grant Company Lunch Counter, 1948. Grant's, at 163 Monroe Avenue, was located in the last surviving structure on what was once known as "Grab's Corners," later called Campau Square. The Bradford House Restaurant, shown here, was famous for its grilled frankfurters. Grant's was initially called "the 25 cent store," and its slogan for many years was "known for values!" (Courtesy Grand Rapids History & Special Collections, Archives, Grand Rapids Public Library.)

KETTLE RINGER OUTSIDE GRANT'S, 1940.
Bradford was the name utilized for house
brands at Grant's, which were manufactured
in Bradford County, Pennsylvania, the
county where founder William T. Grant was
born. Grant's operated at this location from
1930 until it closed in 1973. The company
was liquidated in 1976. This structure
was sold to the city for $300,000 and
demolished as part of the plan to straighten
out Monroe Avenue. (Courtesy Grand
Rapids History & Special Collections,
Archives, Grand Rapids Public Library.)

**F.W. WOOLWORTH COMPANY STORE NO.
45, 1939.** The location at 169 Monroe
Avenue replaced an earlier store on
Monroe Avenue that opened in 1911.
This emporium covered almost 20,000
square feet and featured terrazzo floors,
marble-faced columns, and a 15-foot-
high ceiling. By the 1950s, this location
generated in excess of $1 million in
sales per year. (Courtesy Grand Rapids
History & Special Collections, Archives,
Grand Rapids Public Library.)

HOLIDAY MARQUEE AT WOOLWORTH'S, 1949. For years, Woolworth's was where one would purchase regional souvenirs, goldfish, holiday decor, yarn, nylons, and cosmetics. House brands included University, Herald Square, Fifth Avenue, Blue Banner, and Lord Madison. Sadly, this location closed in 1979, ending over 65 years of dime store presence on this block. (Courtesy Grand Rapids History & Special Collections, Archives, Grand Rapids Public Library.)

Visit us at
arcadiapublishing.com